Going Down to the Sea

Going Down to the Sea

CHINESE SEX WORKERS ABROAD

Ko-lin Chin

 Silkworm Books

ISBN: 978-616-215-077-7

First published in 2014 by
Silkworm Books
6 Sukkasem Road, T. Suthep
Chiang Mai 50200 Thailand
info@silkwormbooks.com
www.silkwormbooks.com

Cover photo by James Felix
Typeset in Minion Pro 10 pt. by Silk Type

Printed in Thailand by O.S. Printing House, Bangkok

5 4 3 2 1

Contents

Acknowledgments

I would like to express my gratitude to the many people who helped me with the research that is the basis for this book. First, I thank all the Chinese sex workers who agreed to take part in my research and who willingly shared their stories with me. I owe my deepest thanks to these women, who are anonymous except for the pseudonyms here. Second, I am grateful to the various operators in the sex trade (agents, escort agency owners, mommies, brothel keepers, etc.) who not only let me talk to them, but also let me enter their world and see how they operate their businesses. Again, I can only thank them anonymously.

I owe a debt of gratitude to my family and friends. I thank Huilin (a cousin), her husband C. Y. Shaw, and their son Rui Shaw for helping me in Singapore. In Hong Kong, I was assisted by Ah Ping (another cousin). I would also like to thank my friends: Yulan Chu, Chuanqiang Zhao, and Guanxuan Cao in Macau; Tiva Jentriacharn in Bangkok; Philip Tien, Benny Phan, and Ferry Siddharta in Jakarta; Punky Pang in Kuala Lumpur; and Wei Chen and Jimeng Tang in China. I thank Robert Chu and his wife Jinfeng Gao in Vancouver. In the United States, Meilan (my sister) and her husband Frank Su offered their help when I was in Los Angeles.

Among the many individuals from the academic community who offered me their invaluable help, I am especially indebted to Yiu Kong

Chu of the University of Hong Kong, Chuen-Jim Sheu of the National Taipei University, Pei-Ling Wang of Jinan University, Shu-Lung Yang of the National Chung Cheng University, Sandy Yu-Lan Yeh of the Central Police University, Narayanan Ganapathy of National Singapore University, Sheldon Zhang of San Diego State University, Mohd Kassim Noor Mohamed of Birmingham City University, Yong Wang and Changrong Zhang of the Fuzhou Police Academy, and Jody Miller of Rutgers University. I am also grateful to Professor James O. Finckenauer, my colleague and partner on this research project, for his enormous contribution to the successful completion of the project.

My sincere gratitude goes to Trasvin Jittidecharak of Silkworm Books for helping me to get this book published. I am also grateful to Judy Mellecker and Joel Akins for editing the manuscript and suggesting ways to improve it.

The research project was supported by a grant from the National Institute of Justice, of the US Department of Justice. I thank Karen Bachar, Jennifer Hanley, and John Picarelli of the National Institute of Justice for their support.

Finally, but most importantly, I would like to thank my wife, Catherine, for her encouragement and patience throughout the course of this project. Without her full support and understanding, this study would not have been completed. This book is dedicated to her.

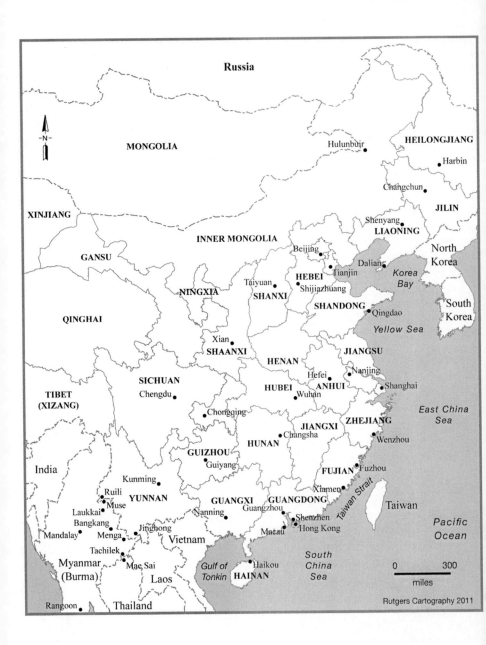

Prologue

Deciding to Interview Chinese Sex Workers

I am a criminal justice professor in the United States whose research expertise concerns transnational organized crime. I have written several books, covering topics such as Chinese gangs and organized crime groups in the United States, the clandestine immigration of Chinese citizens to America, the penetration of gangsters into business and politics in Taiwan, and the drug trade in the Golden Triangle in Southeast Asia. Over the past thirty years, I have conducted face-to-face interviews with street gang members, mafia figures, illegal immigrants, human smugglers, drug addicts, and drug dealers in their own environments, without the presence of a third party and unconstrained by law enforcement authorities. Besides formally interviewing my subjects, I have also spent many hours eating, drinking, and chatting with my subjects in streets, restaurants, bars, and various entertainment venues in the hope that these activities would offer me a better understanding of my subjects and their lives.

In the 1980s and 1990s, social, economic, and political changes around the world led to the massive movement of people across international borders. Of these migrants, many were women and children believed to have been trafficked from one country to another for the purpose of

1

sexual or labor exploitation. According to various NGOs and advocacy groups, many of the women and children desperate to go overseas to make money are vulnerable to criminals who often use deception, force, and coercion to transport victims across borders so that they can be used for cheap labor or as sex slaves.

Before long, the problem of human trafficking attracted the attention of the US government. In 2000, a new federal law, the Trafficking Victims Protection Act (TVPA), directed the US Department of State to establish the Office to Combat and Monitor Trafficking in Persons. The Office, led by an ambassador-at-large, is responsible for collecting information about human trafficking around the world. It publishes an annual report (called the TIP report) evaluating how various nations deal with the issue. The report groups and ranks all countries of interest in tiers (Tier 1, Tier 2, Tier 2 Watch List, Tier 3) based upon the extent of their efforts to fight human trafficking. The report is a tool for the US government to "name and shame" foreign governments in the hope that they will prosecute traffickers, protect victims, and prevent human trafficking. Pursuant to the TVPA, the US government may withhold foreign assistance that is neither humanitarian nor trade-related to countries in Tier 3.

The Office also spends hundreds of millions of dollars every year to fund a variety of programs across the world to identify and rescue trafficked victims and to prevent human trafficking. Some of these programs have involved the establishment of shelters for rescued victims and initiatives to help victims start a new life either in receiving or sending countries. Many countries have also followed the example of the United States by passing their own antitrafficking laws and allowing victims to remain in the receiving country if they are willing to help the authorities prosecute the traffickers.

However, between 2000 and 2010, only a few hundred trafficked victims were identified and rescued in the United States, even though US authorities had estimated that around 45,000 victims were trafficked into the country every year. Why such a huge discrepancy? Some researchers believed that human traffickers were extraordinarily shrewd criminals who knew how to hide their victims and control them through threats and violence. But other observers were skeptical and contended that very few people were actually being trafficked; on the contrary, most migrants who went overseas to work did so voluntarily and were not being exploited or controlled.

To find out who was right, I decided to conduct an empirical study.[1] My plan was to interview women who worked in the sex trade (*xaihai* or "going down to the sea")[2] overseas, in order to ask them whether they were deceived or coerced when they went abroad to engage in commercial sex. I also decided to interview women only from mainland China, for two reasons: (1) communication—since I speak Chinese, there would be no language problems; and (2) resources—limiting the number of subjects and situations would be an efficient use of time and money.

Locating Chinese Sex Workers

I also spent some time thinking about the destination countries to be included in my study and eventually decided that I would do research only in the following countries and special administrative regions in China: Hong Kong, Macau, Taiwan, Thailand, Malaysia, Singapore, Indonesia, and the United States. Hong Kong and Macau are located on the Chinese mainland; when Britain and Portugal returned them to China in 1997 and 1999, respectively, China began to allow its citizens to travel to these two special administration regions. Before long, Chinese women began to show up in Hong Kong and Macau to engage in commercial sex. At one point, many of the streets of Hong Kong and Macau were occupied by streetwalkers known as "women from the north." Several movies about the plight of Chinese sex workers in Hong Kong also came out at that time.

In the early 1990s, many people from the coastal areas of China—especially men living in Fujian Province—were smuggled into Taiwan by boat to work as laborers. A few years later, fewer male migrants from China were going to Taiwan, but more Chinese women were showing up on the island to work in the sex industry. After the Taiwanese authorities began to crack down on the maritime smuggling of Chinese women into Taiwan, sex ring operators in Taiwan relied on fake marriages to bring Chinese women into Taiwan. Soon the sex trade in Taiwan was dominated by women known as "mainland sisters."

In Southeast Asia, Thailand is both a major tourist destination and a country with a well-developed sex industry. Many women from outside Thailand have arrived to work in the sex trade. Among these foreign women, many from China can be seen working in the numerous entertainment venues located in and around Bangkok's Chinatown.

Thailand is a Buddhist country, whereas Malaysia and Indonesia are Muslim countries. However, these three countries all have sizeable Chinese populations. Besides the local-born Chinese, there are also many Chinese from Hong Kong, Taiwan, and the mainland visiting these three countries as tourists, businesspeople, and workers. The Chinese diasporas in these three countries became the main sources of customers for the Chinese sex workers there.

There are also many US-born Chinese in the United States, as well as large numbers of old and new Chinese immigrants. Chinese sex workers in the United States mainly cater to Chinese immigrants. Most Chinese live in New York or Los Angeles; for this reason, I included these two American cities in my study.

Of course, Chinese sex workers can be found in many other countries. There are quite a few of them in Myanmar (Burma), South Korea, and Japan, and a smaller number in the Philippines, Australia, Cambodia, and in countries in Europe, the Middle East, and Africa. I decided to exclude all these countries because I had limited time and resources.

Gaining Cooperation

I have interviewed many hard-to-reach subjects in the past and initially thought it would not be a difficult task to approach sex workers for an interview. These women are everywhere if you are looking, so how difficult could it be to find them? Only later did I learn that while it is not much of a problem to locate them, it is a challenge to persuade them to be interviewed. Many big-time gangsters, human smugglers, and drug kingpins are surely not willing to attract public attention, but at the same time they are not ashamed of who they are, and some of them are not so reluctant to talk to a college professor. However, no woman is willing to admit that she is a sex worker, unless she is working and the person in front of her is a potential client. A Chinese sex worker in Jakarta said something like this when I asked her for advice on how to find and persuade women in the sex trade to be interviewed: "Heck! No woman is going to tell no one she is selling her ass."

Regardless, my plan was to interview fifteen to eighteen women at each of the nine sites. I also wanted to interview women from a variety of sex venues: hostesses in nightclubs or KTVs,[3] "technicians" (a popular term in China for masseuses) in well-established saunas or spas, masseuses in small massage parlors, prostitutes in brothels, escorts from outcall agencies, and streetwalkers or independent sex workers seeing clients in hotels or apartments.

Between December 2006 and May 2008, I traveled to the nine research sites and personally interviewed 149 sex workers. Why were these women willing to talk to me? There were many reasons—the first and most important was that they trusted me with their stories. I was not going to reveal their identities. I did not ask them their real names, their home addresses in China, nor did I take their pictures or tape-record their interviews. They were assured that the interviews would be anonymous and that no one could link the completed questionnaires to them. To make my subjects feel at ease, I dressed very simply: shorts and a T-shirt. I also did not carry any recording device with me. If anyone was especially worried, I lifted my T-shirt, turned around, and then emptied my pockets to show that I was not carrying or wearing any electronic video or audio devices. Of course, doing these things in an exaggerated and funny way often helped to lighten things up. Sometimes I would show them my US passport to make the point that it was highly unlikely I was also a local cop or a reporter. (In general, these women were most concerned about running into a police officer or a journalist.)

Another way to persuade them to participate in my study was to pay them what they charged their customers for a session. Some of my subjects only allowed their customers thirty minutes per session; under such circumstances, I paid them for two sessions so that I would have one hour to conduct the interview. For many sex workers, "hitting a wall" (not seeing any client the whole day) is the most frustrating (and humiliating if noticed by coworkers) thing to endure, so as long as someone is willing to play the role of a paying client, they are more than happy to accommodate.

Most of the women I approached were at first suspicious of my motives, despite the many times I assured them that I really was a scholar from the United States and would do nothing to harm them. I had the feeling that most subjects became more open after talking to me for a while, and that was because I did not ask them questions that were too sensitive or embarrassing to answer. I also treated them with respect and believe they could tell from my interactions with them that I was not making judgments towards them or their profession. I think these were crucial factors in their willingness to talk to me.

To encourage these women to talk freely, I did not even carry a pen or a sheet of paper, not to mention a questionnaire. I did prepare a standardized questionnaire to make sure all the subjects were asked the same set of questions, so that I would be able to compile a quantitative data file for statistical analysis in the future. There were fifty-one questions in my questionnaire, and I memorized all of them so that when I was with a subject I was able to "turn on" the "tape recorder" in my mind: I would ask one question after another and also remember all the answers. After an interview, I would go back to my hotel room as soon as possible and write down all the answers in a blank questionnaire.

Of course, this was an imperfect approach. I may have forgotten to ask some of the questions, and sometimes I may have forgotten some of the answers or remembered them incorrectly. However, I believe I did not forget any of the important questions, and I was very careful when remembering numbers, like the subject's age, number of visits to a particular destination country, charge per session, and so on. I could not remember the subjects' answers word-for-word. I had to write the answers based on my memory.

When I was in the field, I remained fully alert to the many ethical issues that might arise while doing this kind of ethnographic fieldwork. I believe the unique opportunity to gain firsthand knowledge about the inner workings of the sex trade more than outweighed any potential ethical concerns that might have arisen, and I am confident that my fieldwork neither facilitated the business of the sex ring operators I was studying nor put my female subjects in harm's way.

I also did not deceive my subjects. Once I was alone with a female subject, I immediately told her who I was and why I was there. I then told her the key points in the verbal informed consent statement, emphasizing that (1) participation was completely voluntary, (2) refusal to participate would involve no penalty or loss of benefit, (3) even if consenting to participate, the subject could refuse to answer any question she wished to, and (4) the subject could terminate the interview at any time. No interviews were conducted without the subject's full consent and understanding of the process. If a woman said no to my request for an interview, I did not pressure her to change her mind.

In Their Own Words

In 2009, I, along with my colleague and research partner Professor James O. Finckenauer, began to analyze the data and write an academic book on the realities of prostitution and global sex trafficking.[4] While working on that book, I felt that I should present the stories of the Chinese sex workers in their own words to the general public as well. The public often reads about sex trafficking in the newspapers, but unfortunately these news reports can sometimes be misleading. I thought that one of the best ways to understand the problem would be to listen to the stories told by the women themselves. It is also my intention to let people outside the academic community have a glimpse of how one college professor went about conducting ethnographic fieldwork on the sensitive issue of prostitution and sex trafficking.

CHAPTER 1

Offering the Girlfriend Experience

KITTY IN HONG KONG

Date: August 21, 2007
Place: An apartment on Nathan Road, Hong Kong
Name: Kitty
Age: 20
Marital Status: Single

Born in a village about two hours' drive from Chongqing. Brought to Chongqing by boyfriend to engage in prostitution. First came to Hong Kong in May 2007, now is here for the second time.

"I really do not like this work."

~

Looking for Sex Workers on the Internet

After I arrived in Hong Kong and told a sociology professor there that I was looking for Chinese sex workers to interview, he gave me the name of a website and told me to check it out. I did, and there I found details about hundreds of young Chinese women, including names, phone numbers, and close-up photos. I spent some time browsing through the information and decided to get in touch with a woman named Kitty.[1] She was introduced as follows:

Name: Kitty
Address: No. xxx, xxx Flat, Nathan Road, Yau Ma Tei, Hong Kong
Phone: xxxx-xxxx
Hours: 24 hours
Age: 20
Height: 1.54 meters
Measurements: 34C-24-34
Nationality: China (Language: Cantonese, Mandarin)
Services: $40[2] DUP + HJ; $50 ML; $65 Full Set[3]

A young and beautiful woman with a sweet smile and an innocent look who can give you the girlfriend experience!

The street where Kitty's place was located—Nathan Road—was not far from my hotel, and it is probably the longest and the best known street in Hong Kong and is always bustling with people. It starts from Tsim Sha Tsui and passes through areas such as Jordan, Yau Ma Tei, Mongkok, and Prince; the whole street is dotted with all kinds of businesses and stores.

Entering a One-Woman Brothel

When I entered the elevator of the building, there was also a middle-aged woman there who appeared to be a resident. When I arrived at the specified floor and was about to exit the elevator, I wasn't sure whether it was the front flat or the rear flat, so I had to ask the woman for directions. After I arrived at the destination, there were two doors and I did not know which one belonged to the brothel.[4] I called the place, and a woman answered the phone. I told her I was standing in front of her door; soon Kitty opened the door and led me through a small living room furnished with a sofa and a TV. The place was relatively clean, and it was also quite bright. There were two rooms inside the apartment; one was locked and she brought me into another room. Her room was extremely small—there was only a massage bed and a small refrigerator. After we walked in, we had to sit on the massage bed because there was nothing else to sit on and not much room to move around.

Kitty had light makeup and long black hair. She was wearing a black night gown, but it was not too revealing. Once Kitty closed the door, I told her right away that I only wanted to interview her for my research project. I explained that I was a professor from the United States and wanted to know why she came to Hong Kong, how she began to engage in prostitution, and her feelings about working in the sex trade. I also assured her that the interview would not be audiotaped or videotaped and that it would be anonymous. Moreover, I told her that I would give her the full set price after the interview, but she also had the right to reject my request, and if she did, I would pay her a little bit of money and leave the premises promptly.

Starting Out

Kitty said yes to my request without much hesitation. She began to answer my questions and did so in a relatively relaxed way.

> I was born in a village about two hours' drive away from Chongqing.[5] I am twenty years old now and I am single. When I was about fourteen years old, I dropped out of school after completing the first year of junior high. My dad is a swindler, specializing in cheating people out of their money; I am not sure how he does that, though. He was once arrested by the police and beaten almost to death. My mom is a housewife, and I have a little sister and a little brother.

Both Kitty and I were sitting on that small massage bed, and it was not a comfortable way to have a long conversation. She paused and changed her position, and I also took the opportunity to adjust mine.

> I worked as a waitress in a restaurant after I dropped out of middle school. I quit after a few days because it was hard work. Then I became an apprentice at a regular hair salon. I was there for more than one year,

and I was not paid at all. After that, I went back to work at a restaurant, met a boy, and had sex with him. My mother slapped me when she found out about this. She also dragged me to a nearby park, all the while crying and yelling, asking me why I was so stupid. She said she would tell my father, who was in another province at that time. I took it hard and fled to another city with a female friend. We checked into a small hotel. I bought ten sleeping pills and swallowed all of them, but I woke up the next morning.

Maybe Kitty was not comfortable sitting with her legs dangling off of the massage bed, so she lifted both her legs on top of the bed.

At that time, all we had left was $3. We took a bus to where my boyfriend lived and he took both of us to a place to sell sex. I wasn't sure what type of sex venue that place was; all I can tell you is that it was a three-story building, the women sit in the lobby on the first floor and wait for customers, and when a man picks a woman, the two of them will go to the second floor to have sex. The charge was $12 per session, and customers were provided food and drinks, too. All the women lived on the third floor.

Not long after, my parents found out my whereabouts, and they brought me home and my dad gave me a good beating. They called the police after they realized I ran away, and that's why the police were looking for me. I remember after my dad beat me up he handcuffed me and wouldn't let me go outside the house.

The phone in the living room rang, startling me a bit because it was very loud and I was concentrating on what Kitty was telling me. She waved her hand, told me not to be bothered, and continued her story.

I was able to run away from home again when my parents were not paying attention. I went to another nearby town and worked in a *falang* [hair salon brothel].[6] At that place, it was $16 per session, and the women received $12. On my way to that town, I called my father and told him I was on my way to Chongqing (actually, I wasn't going there) and asked him to just pretend that he never had a daughter like me. He demanded that I return home right away, but I simply ignored him.

When I was at that hair salon brothel, I hung out with all kinds of people with dubious backgrounds. Each day, I normally saw two or three clients, made about $30, and went out after work and spent all the money I had earned, leaving only $3 for taxi. At that time, I also began to smoke, drink, and take drugs.

From Dongguan to Shenzhen to Hong Kong

As Kitty spoke, the doorbell rang. She said not to be concerned, because both she and her boss were working, so there was no point in opening the door. The person outside seemed to know that there were people inside the apartment, and so the doorbell continued to ring nonstop, forcing us to stop talking. After a while, the person gave up and Kitty continued her story.

> Later, I came to know a man who told me that there's little money to make near Chongqing, and he urged me to go to Guangdong Province. Soon, he brought me to Changping.[7] I got a job as a hostess in a nightclub, but I left after only a few days because I did not like the atmosphere and the services we had to provide. There, we had to treat our customers like emperors, and fulfill all their crazy demands, and I did not like that. The standard prices there were $26 for hostessing, $62 for going out with a customer to have sex, and $100 for spending a night with a customer. All the nightclubs in the Dongguan area basically charged the same amount of money. At that time, the boyfriend who brought me to Dongguan had already gone to Macau, so I contacted a girlfriend who was working in a hair salon brothel in Shenzhen and asked her to let me join her.[8] She and I used to hang out while I was in the Chongqing area; she was brought to Shenzhen by her boyfriend too.

I heard the boss in the next room now moving in the living room, probably after just seeing a client. I also heard the entrance door open and close—perhaps the boss just waving goodbye to her client. I noticed that Kitty began to look a little nervous, probably because she was talking to me without the approval of her boss. When she spoke again, she tried to lower her voice; luckily, the boss turned on the TV in the living room, but she kept the volume fairly low.

After working in that hair salon brothel in Shenzhen for a few days, I was arrested; I was only sixteen. The police were nice to me, asking me why a girl like me would engage in prostitution. I was required to pay a $126 "education fee," and if I didn't, the police in Shenzhen would notify the police in my hometown to ask my family to come up with the money. I didn't want anyone from my village to find out about my arrest, so I wrote a letter begging my parents to send me the money, and they did—promptly.

Originally, I thought I wouldn't be punished after paying the fine, but I was wrong. I was sentenced to a jail in Shenzhen for six months. That jail was only for sex workers. Some of the inmates were in their forties; I was considered to be one of the younger ones, but there was also a fourteen-year-old. Work inside the jail was harsh, and it wasn't easy for me to spend six months in there. By the time I was out, I was seventeen.

After I got out, I returned to the hair salon brothel in Shenzhen. Later, with someone's help, I went back to Dongguan to work in nightclubs, and moved from midlevel nightclubs to high-level ones. By then I had become much more mature, and I began to understand that I should always look for high-end entertainment venues to work in.

Later, a young woman from a nightclub introduced me to someone in Hong Kong. When I was in China, I always dreamed of going to Hong Kong and Macau one day, so when the opportunity was there, I took it. This place is a one-woman brothel. A friend introduced me to the female boss. She treats me very well. She buys me food if I am hungry but too busy to get it myself because I am with a customer. Of course, she is nice to me because I am making money for her.

More than $1,500 in Seven Days

The phone in the living room rang again; I thought the boss was going to answer it, but she didn't. Kitty stopped talking when the phone rang, but she did not act like she was about to go out and answer it.

I came here to Hong Kong on my own, and I did not pay anybody to get here. I applied for a seven-day travel pass myself and crossed the Louhu Checkpoint to enter Hong Kong.[9] When I came here for the first time in May 2007, I worked for only a week but I went back with more than $1,500. When I was working for a nightclub in Dongguan, I made a little more than $375 a week when business was good; if business was slow, I made a little more than $250 a week. This is my second visit to Hong Kong; I just got here the day before yesterday. I am going to work every day while I am here, and after seven days, I have to return to China.

For full service, I get $37 and the boss gets $28. I don't think the way the money from the client is split between me and my boss is fair, but I can also understand that the boss is taking a huge risk in running this type of business.

Every day I begin to work after nine or around ten, and I stop working around nine at night. I sleep in this same room. Once in a while, the boss and I will go out for a walk. When I was here for the first time, I served eighteen customers a day when business was good. Yesterday, I had ten clients. At any rate, I usually have about ten customers a day. My clients are OK; they are well-mannered, so to speak. Anyway, clients here are definitely better than those in China. When business is slow, I will sit in the living room and watch TV. Even though I am free to go outside by myself, I rarely venture out.

Kitty's Boyfriend

Kitty described her daily routine to me with a smile. Soon, she began to tell me about her boyfriend.

After being arrested and spending six months in jail in China, I am terrified with the thought that I could also be arrested by the police here in Hong Kong. You could say I go to work every day with a heavy heart, and that's why after this trip, I may not come back here again but just work in Dongguan instead. My boyfriend also did not want me to come to Hong Kong. He was the one who brought me to Guangdong from Chongqing. I made about $1,500 during my first trip (seven days) and I gave all the money to him. He is twenty-three—not handsome, but I like him. He told me that after one more year, I don't have to work anymore. He used to have a girlfriend who was also a sex worker. Many people warned me that he is not dependable, including my mother. But I won't listen to them. My boss also told me not to give him all my money. But I do. I hope he won't cheat on me.

It was clear Kitty was not so sure about her boyfriend's loyalty, but she tried her best to remain positive.

I really do not know how I ended up working in the sex industry. I still remember when I was learning to be a hairdresser and helping clients to wash their hair, many of our customers were sex workers. At that time, I thought these women were really dirty, and I asked my colleagues in a mocking way how much these women charge their clients per session. After I finished my job of washing hair, I would ask them to buy me something to eat, and if they said yes, I would go get the most expensive items on the menus, thinking these women were loaded anyway. Not in my wildest dreams would I have thought it possible that I might become a sex worker myself one day.

I really do not like this work. Before entering this line of work, a group of sex workers told me that it may be hard to have sex with a stranger for money at the first time, but after a few times, I will get used to it. I don't think it is true, because even now I am totally disgusted with what I am doing.

The boss outside was signaling to us (by knocking on the door but saying nothing) that it was about time for me to leave, because I had been in there for almost an hour. I got up and paid Kitty the $65 that was tucked away in my pocket before I walked in.

When I walked past the living room, I saw the woman boss sitting there and watching TV. She smiled at me, and said in broken Cantonese, "Please visit us again soon." I nodded gently, and walked out of the one-woman brothel.

CHAPTER 2
Sitting Table and Doing "Fast Food"
LING LING IN HONG KONG

Date: August 23, 2007
Place: A hotel in Hong Kong
Name: Ling Ling
Age: 24
Marital Status: Single

Born in Chongqing, went to Yunnan Province to engage in sex work after father lost his business, now living in Changan, Guangdong Province. First arrived in Hong Kong in July 2007; this is her second trip.

"That experience cast a shadow over me for the rest of my life."

~

A Mommy in the Park

After interviewing Kitty, I remembered that when I was in Hong Kong in the summer of 2004, I saw many Chinese women soliciting business in a small park in Tsim Sha Tsui, a major tourist attraction in Kowloon where many upscale stores, restaurants, and hotels are located. I decided to go there to see whether I could find a streetwalker to interview. I got there around nine o'clock at night and did not see even one woman walking the streets. Because of massive police crackdowns in 2005 and 2006, street prostitution in Hong Kong seemed to have been almost completely wiped out. Walking down Shangdong Street and Shanghai Street in Mongkok and Temple Street in Yau Ma Tei two days earlier, I likewise had noticed only a few women who appeared to be in the sex trade. In the past, these streets had been packed with hundreds of young women from China looking for customers.

At the park, after I found a place to sit down, I noticed a woman in her early forties who seemed to be a local. I made eye contact with her when she walked by me a couple of times; then, realizing she was not going to make the first move, I went over and said hello and quickly learned that she was a mommy (madam or mama-san) soliciting business for a group of young women.

She said she was from Laoning Province, had been living in Hong Kong for many years, was divorced, and, because she wanted to make more money than would come from working in a restaurant, had decided to risk becoming a mommy. Her name was Ellen. I told Ellen that I was a professor from the United States doing research for a project on sex workers. That evening, Ellen and I had a long chat. She told me everything about herself and her role as a mommy. While we were talking, she kept an eye on passersby, and if she thought that a particular man was a potential customer, she walked over and asked whether he was looking for a "massage." Business was slow that night; in a little more than an hour, Ellen approached four men but none was looking for a companion. A white couple passed by, and after noticing that Ellen was soliciting business, the male partner (probably in his fifties) pretended to be alone and interested in buying sex. For a while, Ellen was fooled, but when the female partner showed up from nowhere, the male partner said in English something like, "See, I told you so, I am not that old." The couple walked away, laughing hilariously, apparently very satisfied with their little experiment.

When I was about to leave, I gave Ellen some money as promised at the beginning of the conversation. I also asked if she would refer some of her women to me for interviews. Ellen said she would give it a try, and if someone was willing to talk to me, she would call my cell phone.

The next day around six in the evening, Ellen called and said she had found someone who agreed to talk to me. She also said the woman was willing to come to my hotel for the interview. Half an hour later, someone rang my room bell, and when I opened the door, I saw a young woman standing in front of me. She was wearing a T-shirt, three-quarter pants, and no makeup.

Selling Virginity in Kunming

After she walked in, I asked whether she would like to go somewhere else to talk but she said it would be fine to do so in my room. After all, Ellen had already explained to her who I was and what I was up to, so she was not concerned that I might have installed a video or audio device inside my room. For many women who are selling sex, appearing on a TV screen is probably more devastating than being arrested, because there would be a chance that their families and relatives might find out what they have been doing while away from home. After I handed her a bottle of water, she began to tell me her story.

> My name is Ling Ling, and I was born in Chongqing. My father used to be an auto mechanic. Later, he borrowed money to lease a bus and start a small transportation business. But the business failed and he lost a lot of money. Creditors came to our home and asked us to repay them. I am the only child and life was hard when I was young. My mother worked part-time in a variety of manual jobs.
>
> I did not want to study anymore after my father's business collapsed, even though I liked school. At first, I worked as a waitress at a restaurant and made about $25 a month. That was not enough to help my family. So I went to Yunnan with a friend and we both decided to enter the sex trade.
>
> We went to Yiliang in Yunnan Province first, and found work in a nightclub. It was a relatively small business operation; customers come into the premises to pick a woman, and then they go somewhere else to have sex. Customers paid $36 per session to the women, plus $6 to the nightclub owner as a "table fee."

For some young women in China, entering prostitution could be as simple as this: there is a financial problem in the family, and one of the children, usually a daughter, decides to sacrifice herself to help her family. Because the best way to make a lot of money in a short time is to sell sex, she becomes a sex worker.

> I was only eighteen then and still a virgin, and that's why I had to wait for about half a month for a client who was looking for a virgin and willing to pay a high price. I learned later that my first client was a top gangster who often traveled to Myanmar, and I bet he was in the drug business. He paid $880 for that session with me; I got $740 and the brothel the rest. That experience cast a shadow over me for the rest of my life. I remembered that after he closed the door to the room, he jumped all over me right away; there was no foreplay whatsoever. He did that to me twice. When he was on top of me, I cried and cried, so he pressed his hand against my mouth and penetrated me with all his might.

In 2004–5, when I was a visiting scholar in Yunnan Province studying the drug trade between Myanmar and China, I also visited Yiliang, a backwater rife with crime and corruption. I was able to imagine what kind of life Ling Ling must have had while she was there, and the kinds of sex buyers she would have had to deal with in that remote area.

From Yunnan to Changan to Hong Kong

> For my second customer, my price dropped to $300; I got $240 and the store took $60. The third customer paid about $120, and after a few more transactions, I became like everybody else—$36 per session. I was very unhappy working there; the place was not nice and I was not able to make much money. I only had about two customers a day; more often than not, it was one customer a day. Later, a friend suggested that we should go to Changan, Guangdong Province, and that's why after less than a year in Yiliang we moved to Changan.[1]

Ling Ling paused and took a sip of water, and she also took a look at her surroundings.

Changan was much better than Yiliang, and that's because Changan was one of the best-developed towns in China. My friend and I began to work in the nightclubs of five-star hotels in Changan. 70 percent of the customers there were from Taiwan, 10 percent from Hong Kong, 10 percent from Japan, and another 10 percent foreigners (white). There were almost no local customers. In those nightclubs, we charged our customers $24 for hostessing (drinking, singing, and flirting), and we gave the club $2.40. If we went out with the customers, we charged $96 for "fast food" (quick sex) and turned over $12 to the nightclub. If we spend the whole night with a customer, we charged $140 and gave the nightclub $24. In Changan, we made much more money—at least $1,200 a month.

I also had been to Changan a couple of times. It is a big town, with a population of more than six hundred thousand, and is definitely a much better place to work and make money than Yiliang.

After I entered this line of work, I soon began to send money home. When I returned home, I told my mother that I was working as a hostess [equivalent to admitting that she was a sex worker]; otherwise I couldn't explain to her where I got all the money. My mom was not surprised when I told her that, and that's because there are so many females from Chongqing engaged in sex work. Many parents can guess what their daughters are doing far away from home, it's just that they don't want to make a hole in a piece of paper [a local expression for exposing the family to embarrassment], so they turn a blind eye.

It sounded like Ling Ling's decision to tell her mother was not difficult.

Pretty soon, I had repaid all the debts my family owed, and after that, I bought a house. My parents also began to live a comfortable life that was beyond their wildest dreams. Everyday, they go around wining and dining and playing mahjong.[2] They even own a dog!

At this point, Ling Ling was smiling happily.

In Changan, I stopped working for a while after clearing the debts, buying a house, saving some money, and not having any pressure to make money. However, my dad bought another house recently so that I can live in that house after I get married. I am already twenty-four, so they have been hoping that I will marry soon. Buying a second house depleted my savings, and I am concerned that without any cash to spend, it would be a nightmare if one of my parents got sick. That's why I decided to come to Hong Kong to give it a try.

Sitting Table and Doing "Fast Food"

Ling Ling did not blame her parents; she knew that they wished her well in buying the house, but those good intentions also pushed her to continue to work in the sex trade.

> I came here to Hong Kong on my own. I applied for a travel permit for a short visit to Hong Kong; it cost only $5. After arriving here, I found a friend to take me to some nightclubs to work as a hostess. I did not pay that friend any money. I came here for the first time in July 2007, and stayed for seven days. This is my second trip to Hong Kong; I have been here for four days now and will return to China next week.
>
> In the nightclubs, we [the women from China] are also customers, not employees. We go around a few nightclubs in this area, and we buy tickets when we go in. If the police come, we tell them we are customers because we also have bought a ticket to get in. In general, we go to these nightclubs around eight or nine at night. Sitting a table normally takes about two and a half hours, and the customer pays us $66. Deducting $13 for the entry fee, we actually make $53 per table. If we go out with a customer for "fast food," the customer pays $200 and the woman gets $160 (the other $40 will go to the nightclub). If a customer wants to book for the whole night, it costs $400, and we will get $333 (the rest goes to the nightclub).

Ling Ling was talking nonstop, and I tried my best to remember all the numbers she was mentioning.

A few days after I got here, I met Ellen. She told me and the other women that besides sitting table and going out with clients at various nightclubs we should also entertain the customers she refers to us. We agreed. We thought we should maximize our income by engaging in a variety of activities. Because we need Ellen to find us customers, we can only receive $53 from customers she refers to us. Besides Ellen, there are quite a few other mommies in that small park soliciting business for us. Regardless of which mommy finds a customer for us, we get $53 per session; how much she actually charges a customer is none of our business. Of course, if customers give us tips, the tips all belong to us. We do not have chickenheads [slang for pimps; "chicken" rhymes with "prostitute" in Chinese] in Hong Kong.[3]

Now I began to understand why I did not see Chinese women soliciting business in the streets of Hong Kong anymore. The mommies had taken over. If a mommy locates a potential customer, she calls a sex worker and asks her to come over to let the customer take a look. If the customer is satisfied with the woman and the two parties agree on a price, the customer gives the woman his details (hotel, room number, etc.). The woman arrives a short time later. Ling Ling was lucky not to have a chickenhead in Hong Kong; I learned later that if a woman works with the help of a chickenhead, she must give him half of her pay. The chickenhead usually only provides the woman with a place to sleep and $7 a day for meals.

Every day, I get up around noon, eat lunch, and then go back to sleep. I get up again around five or six in the evening and then prepare myself for work. I arrive at the nightclubs around eight or nine, go to the small park around ten or eleven, and go home around two or three in the morning. Every day, if I can sit a table and make $53, and do a "fast food" and get another $53, I am very happy. If a mommy finds a customer who wants to spend the whole night with me, I get $107 plus tip.

When I was here the first time, I stayed for seven days. I made quite a lot of money. After deducting all my expenses for the trip and the money I spent in Hong Kong, my net income in Hong Kong for seven days was about the same as what I would have made in Changan in a month. I made $133 yesterday, $146 the day before yesterday, and $160 the day before that.

Afraid of the Police

Many young women are willing to go overseas to engage in prostitution simply because they can make significantly more money than at home. In Ling Ling's case, her one-week income in Hong Kong was equivalent to her one-month income in Changan. What about the clients in Hong Kong compared to those in China? What were the problems?

> When we are running around the nightclubs, we will have the opportunity to sit one table every evening—sometimes two tables. We rarely have the chance to go out with customers for sex after sitting their tables in the nightclubs. In the small park, we may have one customer per night, or maybe two. Most of the customers we find in the park are foreigners, and they are not as good as the customers in Changan. After all, the two nightclubs I worked for in Changan are both located within five-star hotels.
>
> I am afraid of being arrested. Every day, my heart is jumping when I go to work, especially when I am dealing with the "fast food" clients Ellen and other mommies located for me in that small park. If a customer brings me to an expensive hotel, I feel fine. But if he takes me to a cheap, hourly hotel, I am really worried about police inspections so I usually finish up my job in ten minutes and leave.
>
> I send all my money to my parents, and this is the happiest thing for me to do. All my colleagues said I am a great daughter. Of course, I also spend a lot of money on clothes, handbags, and shoes, and I only buy name-brand.

I asked Ling Ling whether she had run into Chinese women who were tricked or forced into prostitution. She reacted like I was asking her a stupid question.

> I did not meet anyone like this in Guangdong Province, not to mention Hong Kong. If a woman was deceived and brought here, isn't it very

easy to escape in a place like Hong Kong? How can a person be under control here?

At this point, Ling Ling asked me whether she could use the bathroom, and I said of course. Upon her return, I asked her what her plan was for the future.

My future plan is to make more money, buy another house, and rent it out. At one point in the past, I applied for a visa to go to Singapore. I spent about $120 for the application, and it was approved. However, a friend who was applying along with me was not approved, so I did not go. After this trip to Hong Kong, I am going to give it a try again with my friend, and if both of us receive our visa, we will go together to work there. I was once in Thailand for three days, but I wasn't working there.

I had a boyfriend once; he was a pilot. He did not know I was a sex worker; I told him I worked for a foreign company. Later, he met a woman who used to serve in the army, and she was from a very powerful family. My boyfriend wanted to date two women at the same time, but I said no and left him.

Ling Ling smiled when she said that, perhaps pleased at her own independence.

I entered this profession because my father owed a lot of money after his business failed. Before I engaged in this business, I looked down on those women who were selling their bodies, and thought they were really cheap. I thought I would rather have someone beat me to death before I would sleep with a man for money. Who would have thought I would become one of them eventually?

I do not regret entering this line of work, but I somewhat regret that I did not get out of it after I cleared my father's debt and bought a house for my parents. I should have quit sex work then and gone to school to learn something, like computer science or accounting.

Ling Ling sighed, and she looked helpless with her current situation. By then, it was almost eight in the evening—time for her to get ready for work. I got up and handed her an envelope containing $65. Ling Ling took the envelope and said thank you. At the door, she turned back, and said that if I was ever in Changan, I should give her a call and perhaps she could introduce me to her friends in the sex trade.

Macau, a Small Hotel, and Chickenheads

DONG DONG IN MACAU

Date: March 23, 2007
Place: A small hotel on San Maa Lou, Macau
Name: Dong Dong
Age: 20
Marital Status: Single

Born in Changde, Hunan. Parents are farmers. At age seventeen travelled to Shenzhen to engage in commercial sex. Initially wanted to change professions, later was brought to Zhuhai and Macau by a boyfriend to resume prostitution. Currently separated from the boyfriend.

''Now I know that he is not a good person. Anyway, men are all the same—they're all good for nothing.''

~

Sex Work in a Small Hotel

In Macau, beyond the main boulevard where most of the big, modern casinos are located, there is an older community with many small hotels, restaurants, and stores. In the lobbies of those small hotels are many young women looking for customers. I interviewed one of these sex workers, and afterward she suggested that I interview a female named Dong Dong who had been betrayed by her boyfriend. Dong Dong had given all the money she made to her boyfriend, not knowing that he already had a wife. Many of Dong Dong's friends knew her story. Everyone expressed sympathy and at the same time ridiculed her poor judgement. I was curious, and decided to find Dong Dong if I could.

Early the next morning I walked into the same hotel lobby and saw a few young women sitting together on a sofa. The previous night I had seen many more in the lobby; perhaps it was still too early (about ten in the morning) for the rest of the women to be up and come down to the lobby. I asked the women on the sofa if Dong Dong was present. I was in luck: Dong Dong identified herself. One of the other women said, "Wow, you're really famous now!" Dong Dong ignored her and simply led me to her room on the second floor. Later, Dong Dong explained that the previous night she did not work, so she had come down to the lobby early to wait for customers.

Her room was very small and dark, with a few pieces of cheap furniture. I told her I just wanted to chat with her but would pay her what she charges nonetheless. She promptly agreed. I explained to Dong Dong who I was and what research I did, and that I had to be sure that she was participating in my study voluntarily.

The Carefree Young Woman from Changde

Dong Dong wore a low-cut shirt and a denim mini-skirt. She sat on the bed, and I sat in a chair facing her. I started to listen to her story.

> I was born in 1987 in Changde, Hunan. My parents worked on a farm. I have an older sister. After dropping out of middle school, I worked in a relative's factory in Changde. I was only thirteen then. Later, I went to work in another factory. I also went to Jiangsu Province to work, also in a factory. After returning to Changde, I stayed home for a while and eventually decided to go to Shenzhen. Before I left for Shenzhen, I had already made up my mind to be a sex worker. It was a decision I made on my own.

In previous interviews, one woman I interviewed in Hong Kong had been helped to enter prostitution by someone else, and another subject, also in Hong Kong, had gone overseas to engage in sex work because her family had debts. But Dong Dong did not have any outside influence; she made up her mind to be a sex worker and just did it.

I was seventeen years old when I left for Shenzhen. The first time I did this type of work was at a upscale nightclub. At the time, it was $60 to be "onstage" [sitting table or hostessing] but $120 to $240 to be "offstage" [leaving the nightclub to spend the night with customers]. At that time, I could make up to $360 every day, but I didn't work every day. Even if the mommy called me for work, I could make up lots of excuses not to go. So at that time, I would work a few days, then rest a few days. I would spend all the money and didn't save up anything.

Dong Dong did not have any financial obligations, so naturally she was carefree. She worked when she wanted to and spent all that she earned.

Pimp Boyfriend

I was a hostess in Shenzhen for two years. Then I decided to go back to my hometown to have a normal life because I was sick of being a hostess. However, I met a man in Changde who was a chickenhead [pimp] and I liked him. He told me one day after we had been together for half a year that he lost money in his business and needed money to pay the debt. He wanted me to help him and suggested I go to Zhuhai and work as a hostess.[1] So I went to Zhuhai and worked in a nightclub. Shortly after arriving in Zhuhai, he sent me to Macau.

My first time in Macau was in February 2006. It was my boyfriend who helped me apply for the business visa. It was valid for one year. Each time I came to Macau, I could stay for up to three months and after one year, I could renew the visa. It's not easy to get this type of visa, but once I had it, I don't know how many times I went back and forth between Zhuhai and Macau.

My boyfriend was also from Changde, twenty-eight years old; he's never been to Macau because he doesn't have the travel documents.

The first time I traveled here from Zhuhai, I was accompanied by a woman who worked in the sex trade here. After arriving, we came straight to this hotel.

Initially, I was still on good terms with my boyfriend and gave him all the money I earned. And he didn't say that I owed him anything. But when I said I wanted to break up with him (after finding out he was married), he said that I owed him $12,700. I began paying him that money, but I still owe him $2,500.

Now I know that he is not a good person. Anyway, men are all the same—they're all good for nothing. I really regret meeting him. Otherwise, I'd already be "ashore" [would have quit the sex business]. I wouldn't be in this situation.

Dong Dong did not have any particular expression. Perhaps she knew that there was no point in regretting.

After arriving at this hotel and renting a room, I started coming down to the lobby and waiting for customers. When I first arrived, business was good because I was a newcomer. There would be more than ten customers every day. There are six floors, and it's very rare for customers to actually rent the rooms. Some women have a room to themselves; some share the room with another woman. Now there are about twenty individuals in the hotel. Work hours are completely liberal. When there's a customer, you take them to the room, $27 for a thirty-minute session. We don't need to give the hotel additional money, as long as we pay $40 on weekdays and $46 to $53 on weekends as room fees.

No wonder the owner of the hotel let these young women rent the rooms. He could charge high rates and rent out most of the rooms. The owner's overhead costs were very limited as well because the hotel staff did not have to provide many services to the hotel "guests."

Customers and Cops

I normally work until morning, around nine o'clock, and then go to sleep until eight o'clock in the evening when I wake up to go to work.

We have freedom, but it's rare for us to go out. If we're really familiar with the customers, then we may go to their hotel to have sex.

Daily business is hard to predict; when it's good, there are more than ten clients a day; when it's bad, only a few. Most of the customers are from Macau, but there are also men from Hong Kong, Taiwan, Japan, Korea, and Singapore, and also white foreigners. Aside from local customers, the next largest group is mainland Chinese. Among them, some are chickenheads from northeast China. If the customer is from Singapore, Japan or Korea, we charge $40, foreigners $65.

And how do tourists find this small hotel? Usually it is because of media reports describing this small hotel with beautiful women in the lobby. I asked Dong Dong about her customers, and she said there were some bad ones too.

I was assaulted by a client. I had a customer who was a chickenhead from northeast China. He asked me to wash my face because he did not like my heavy makeup. I refused, and he mumbled a few words about my bad attitude. After sex, he asked me whether it was okay for him to not pay me. I said, "Hell, no!" I also said if he didn't pay, I would call the police. He said go ahead, so I picked up the phone. He then hit me. I was deeply hurt by what he did. Eventually, he paid me $27 and left.

Dong Dong looked indignant and seemed to express self-pity. Every woman who recalled a pimp from northeast China seemed to have had similar negative experiences.

Despite having been deceived by her pimp and given the runaround, whenever she encounters the police, Dong Dong's ability to handle the situation is quite good.

In Macau, I have been questioned twice by the police, both times in the lobby of this hotel. I was released shortly after the first arrest. Not long after, the police came to the hotel again and requested my documents. When the police requested my documents, I told them they were in Beijing so that I could apply for a visa to go to Singapore. Actually, my visa was in the hotel room, and the police knew it was in my room. But they didn't go to the room, and after a while, they just left.

Hunanese vs. Northeastern Chickenheads

At this hotel, about 80 percent of the women are from Changde [Hunan]. Others are from northeast China [including the provinces of Liaoning, Jilin, and Heilongjiang] or Sichuan Province. Most of the women here have pimps; those without are rare. The pimps are from Hunan or the northeast. Those from Hunan are a little better than those from the northeast; they won't force women to take customers nonstop. Once, there was a northeast woman here who was not pretty enough to have any business. Her chickenhead hit her, wouldn't let her sleep, and forced her to work twenty-four hours a day. Every day, she was waiting for business in the lobby with blackened eyes. These pimps are not human beings.

Those days going in and out of Dong Dong's small hotel, I would observe one or two men sitting in the corner of the lobby. Apparently, they were the pimps. At times, I would stare at them a little longer, and they would stare back too.

Also, the pimps from Hunan have romantic relationships with their women, whereas the pimps from the northeast have only a financial relationship with the women. Northeast pimps come to this hotel frequently to buy sex. Before they come to the hotel, they have already used drugs, so they won't ejaculate for a long time. Now, when we see them, we don't want to serve them and tell them we don't have any rooms for them. Or we tell them we have our periods and can't have sex with them. Then they yell all kinds of profanity at us. Anyway, we don't want their business.

Macau's Shark Tank

After working at this hotel for some time, I also worked a five-star hotel for a while. If I go and request a room at that hotel, the manager will give me a "service girl room," that means I am in business—I can see clients in my room. You can't do business in a regular room. "Service girl rooms" are more expensive than regular rooms. I would pay $126 per night on weekdays and $173 per night on weekends. There was a lot of pressure there, but the reason I stopped was because we had to find customers in the basement shopping arcade. In order to get customers, I walked around the shopping arcade for a couple of days—all my toes were swollen up into balls. I had to walk so much every day, I couldn't endure it; besides, there were a lot of perverted customers there. But these perverted customers also tend to be generous. They tip a lot. Strange, it's like the more perverted a customer is, the more money he has. At the big five-star hotel, I didn't need a pimp there to approve anything, and the women there also didn't treat me as an outsider. But the hotel's rules were very strict: you can't wear jeans, you can't be too exposed, you have to wear more elegant clothing.

This five-star hotel is famous in Macau. The locals call the basement shopping arcade of the hotel the "Shark Tank." A lot of young women walk around, and when they see male customers, they ask, "Do you want to go?" They are like sharks—circling around, hunting for their prey. This is also one of Macau's major tourist attractions; many visitors (mostly male) come just to watch the action.

Actually, the money I make in Macau is not that much more than in Shenzhen. I can make more in Macau than in Zhuhai though. In that case, why do I not return to Shenzhen? There are two main reasons. First, I am afraid that I'll bump into someone I know. My family doesn't know that I am a sex worker. Second, in Shenzhen, the police have tighter controls, and if caught, there's a possibility of a six-month jail term.

I worked for one month in Singapore. It was at Lorong [lane] 10 in Geylang. At the time, I would make $50 per session, give $6 to the pimp, then another $6 as protection fee. There are some pimps who were very mean, but my pimp treated me fairly well. There, I could have more than ten customers per day. It was October 2006 then. I've also been to Malaysia and stayed in the Genting Highlands [a popular resort area not far from Kuala Lumpur]. I only stayed for four days then left because there were three pimps who treated the women extremely well, and we suspected they were up to something bad against us, so we quickly left. Not long afterwards, a Chinese woman was murdered. Also, lots of Chinese sex workers have been robbed in Malaysia. There was also a case in Genting when, after their meeting, a male customer pulled a gun on the woman and took all of her money. The four days I was there, I gambled every single day, even though my goal was to go there and make money. I would tell customers to wait for me until I finished gambling, and they would actually wait for me. How funny!

At this point in the conversation, Dong Dong started to laugh.

I am living day by day now; I don't have any plans for the future. I just want to repay all the debt I owe my pimp, then save up some money, go back home, and start a small business. And I want to find someone to marry me.

After finishing the talk, I gave Dong Dong $54 (the price for two sessions), and she accompanied me downstairs.

CHAPTER 4

Deluxe Style in a Sauna

RUBY IN MACAU

Date: March 27, 2007
Place: A sauna on Beijing Street, Macau
Name: Ruby
Age: 21
Marital Status: Single

Born in a village near Chongqing. Began to engage in prostitution in a hair salon in Guangzhou at age seventeen. Later, boyfriend (a chickenhead) sold her to another chickenhead. Currently working in a sauna in Macau, waiting for opportunity to work in a nightclub.

"I did not want to make it hard on myself by working in a factory, so I became a sex worker."

～

Looking for Someone from a Sauna to Interview

Shortly after arriving in Macau, I went down to the sauna located inside the hotel where I was staying. A young female manager brought me to a sofa in the corner (a waitress promptly brought me a cup of tea) and explained that it cost about $20 for "pure sauna," an entry fee that allows a customer to use all the facilities inside the premise; regular massage cost about $50, half set $70, and full set at least $150 plus 15 percent tax. For full set, there were Vietnamese-style, European-style, Taiwanese-style, and so on. I calculated that $150 plus 15 percent tax would be nearly $175, over three times more than my budget of $50 per subject. So I told the manager I would be back, and left.

Later, I passed by another sauna located not far away from my hotel. (In fact, there were many saunas near my hotel, some of them inside large hotels and some inside commercial buildings. The ones inside the large hotels tended to be bigger and more expensive than those in the commercial buildings.) This one was also inside an upscale hotel. I took the elevator to the third floor, where a male manager greeted me at the elevator door. When I walked into a waiting area, there were already two male Chinese-speaking visitors waiting for an opportunity to take a look at the women. The manager immediately asked all the young women in the sauna to come out and stand in a line. There were about thirty of them. The manager told us where each group of sex workers came from. The largest group, about a dozen women, came from China. The women in this group were further categorized into two subgroups, one of which cost more than the other. The rest of the groups came from Vietnam, South Korea, Japan, Mongolia, and Russia. There was also one from Italy.

A customer quickly picked a woman from South Korea, and once the manager announced her number, she turned around and disappeared into a back room, probably to prepare herself for work. The other man shook his head and said he did not like any of the masseuses. I shook my head, too. The manager then dismissed all the women. When the manager was explaining to us where the women came from, he also told us what the charges were. The prices were high—between $150 and $185. The Korean woman who was picked cost $185. The manager asked the man who picked her to go over to a counter and pay before going inside. The other man and I turned around and left.

Eventually, after a couple of false starts, I found a sauna not far from my hotel, located inside a commercial building. There was a small counter on the sidewalk, where a young woman was urging male passersby to come inside. The charges were reasonable, so I decided to go in and give it a try.

Deluxe Style, Romantic Style, Freedom Style

The sauna was located in the basement of the building, right across from a nightclub. Inside the sauna, there was a counter and a waiting area, a changing room, a pool, and two steam rooms. I changed into a bathrobe and went to a lounge area with dozens of easy chairs and several large flat-screen TVs on the walls. All the waitresses were from Indonesia and all the masseuses were from China, the latter wearing bikinis.

Visitors can watch TV, play electronic games, or use computers to access the Internet. Visitors can also eat and drink for free. The place was open twenty-four hours a day. I found a place to lie down, and, like the others, I ordered a cold drink and some food. Not long after, a male manager came over to me and explained the kinds of services available and their prices:

> Here, there are three kinds of prices for full-set service. The first is Deluxe Style, which costs $70, but you cannot choose the woman; the second is Romantic Style, costs $100, and you select from a small group of women; the third is Freedom Style, costs $125, and you can select anyone you want, just like picking a woman in a pageant contest.[1]

It was not even five in the evening when the manager first approached me, so those were the daytime prices. After five, all the prices would go up somewhat. I told the manager I wanted to finish my meal first; he said fine and left me there.

Two Chinese men were ready to select a masseuse for themselves. Once the manager learned that the men wanted Freedom Style women, he ordered all the young women from that category to stand in front of the men. Of the roughly twenty women who showed up, the men selected two, who subsequently lay down alongside the men and began to whisper into their ears. The women also began to feed the men fruit from a plate. About fifteen minutes later, the men and the women went inside, where the back rooms were located.

After I finished my meal, I decided to interview a Deluxe Style woman so that I wouldn't go too far over my budget. When the manager learned that I wanted a less costly masseuse, he did not pressure me to pick a more expensive woman. A worker took me to a back room that contained a bed and bathroom. The place was quite clean. Soon, a young woman walked in and introduced herself as Ruby. She then went into the bathroom and was about to prepare the bath for me, but I asked her to sit down and chat with me. She was apparently nervous when I said that, but she sat down as I asked. I told her in detail who I was, what I was doing there, and what I would like her to do. She listened carefully and without much hesitation said she would help the best she could.

Entering Prostitution

Ruby began to tell me her story in a friendly tone.

> I am twenty-one, single. I graduated from middle school. I was born in a rural area near Chongqing; it takes about an hour by car from Chongqing to my village. All my neighbors were farmers. My parents, too. I have an elder brother, and as far as I can remember, my family was doing fine when I was a child.

A waitress knocked on the door and asked me what I would like to drink. I ordered a cup of tea.

> I started a small business after middle school and also worked as a babysitter. Either way, I could not make more than $36 a month. I went to Guangzhou when I was just seventeen, and found a job in a hair salon there. I knew there was special service [selling sex] in the salon. I did not want to make it hard on myself by working in a factory, so I became a sex worker. At the hair salon, I made more than $12 per session.

Ruby was telling me all this calmly, and it seemed like she did not give much thought to her decision to enter the world of prostitution at the age of seventeen. At that point, the waitress returned with my tea. She saw Ruby and I sitting there talking, and she appeared to be very curious about what was going on.

> After working in the hair salon for a while, a client in his twenties took me to Zhongshan, where we lived together for about a year.

Then I discovered he was sleeping with another woman. We had a big argument. He got very angry and sold me to another man. I do not know how much he got—probably about $500.

I tried my best to memorize and make sense of what Ruby told me, but there were a few things I was not able to fully understand.

The man who bought me was in his thirties, and he brought me to Shenzhen and put me to work in sex venues such as KTVs and hair salon brothels. I also became his girlfriend later, and he gambled away all my earnings. A year later, he let me go, and I went back to Chongqing. I came to Macau from Chongqing. I did not tell anyone at home that I was in Macau; they thought that I was back in the Guangdong area.

In Chongqing, I came to know a woman who had been working in a nightclub in Macau. I was not able to save any money after working for almost four years in the sex industry in China. Of course, part of the reason was because my boyfriend was gambling away all my earnings. She told me that I can make more in Macau. Besides, I wouldn't be arrested in Macau for prostitution. She brought me here. I applied for a passport and other travel documents myself, so I did not have to spend much money. The two of us took a train from Chongqing to Zhuhai, and crossed the Gongbei Checkpoint to Macau.

Learning to Do "Ice and Fire"

Some women, especially those who were brought to Macau by their chickenheads, needed to pay several thousand US dollars to come to Macau. Ruby was lucky; she did not have to spend a lot of money because a friend helped her.

We looked for an apartment after arriving here. My friend and I are living together now; we share the rent, it is more than $400 a month. I went to the nightclub where she works, but the manager told me I was a little heavy, so he did not hire me. So I came to this sauna; I was hired right away but told I would be a regular masseuse—not pretty enough to be a member of the pageant team.

Before I started to work, people in the sauna taught me massage. For the "ice and fire" technique (oral sex with cold, then warm water in the mouth), they gave me a video tape to watch. After watching the tape, I knew how to do it. I also had to pay $150 for the "uniform" that includes a bikini and a pair of shoes. Furthermore, I pay $3 a day as some kind of fee, and it covers one meal.

Ruby was smiling when she was talking about the "ice and fire" technique and the $150 "uniform."

I can come to work anytime between 11:00 a.m. and 6:00 p.m., then usually work until 6:00 a.m., but I can go home before that if I want. We watch TV, rest, or sleep if there is no business. My friend comes back around the same time I do.

I was surprised to learn that the masseuses could report to work anytime between 11:00 a.m. and 6:00 p.m. and leave early if they felt like it. Ruby, however, was not free to move around the lounge area like the women in the Romantic Style and Freedom Style groups.

I see two or three clients a day. They are mainly from Hong Kong, Taiwan, and China. They are okay, but some of them are not easy to please. A few days ago, I met a man from the Middle East and I could not communicate with him. He was really difficult to serve. He hit my buttock and thigh with his hand with such force when he was on top of me. Most clients do not resist when we use our mouths to put on their condoms, some will even take the initiative and ask us about wearing condoms, but not this Middle East man. That guy also stuck his fingers into my ass; what a sick man!

My only concern working here is not able to make money, nothing else. Police won't come to this place. Here, a client pays $70 or $100 per session. Before 5:00 p.m., it's $70; after that, it's $100. I only receive $33 per session. If I do two sessions a day, I am not making much money. I only hope I can lose some weight and then find a job at a nightclub.

I left China with a tourist visa to Thailand, so I can stay in Macau for fourteen days on my way to Thailand. After fourteen days, if I return to China and come back here, I can stay for another seven days. After that, I must go to Thailand, but on my way back, I can stay in Macau for another fourteen days.

Finally, I asked Ruby what her plan was for the future.

I do not have any particular take on being a sex worker; I feel fine as long as I get used to it. All I am thinking now is to make enough money, go back to Chongqing, and find a man to marry me.

As time was running out, I finished the interview and returned to the lounge area.

An Agent, a Jockey, and a Fake Husband
MI MI IN TAIWAN

Date: February 10, 2007
Place: An apartment in Taichung, Taiwan
Name: Mi Mi
Age: 28
Marital Status: Single

Born in Yongzhou, Hunan. Entered sex work in Dongguan when she was eighteen; also worked in the Hong Kong sex industry. First arrived in Taiwan in June 2005; this is her second visit.

"I told her I know all these gimmicks; no big deal!"

The "Company" in Taiwan

There are many legitimate adult entertainment venues in Taiwan, but it is difficult to find women from mainland China working in these establishments. Even if I could locate someone, getting her to talk to me would be almost impossible anyway because these women want to protect themselves and their employers from the local authorities. I asked a PhD student of mine (herself a police officer) to introduce me to a Taiwanese police officer who was well connected to the sex ring operators there. That is how I met Peter, the owner of an escort agency.

In Taiwan, someone who pays to bring women from China to Taiwan is called *jinji* (agent) and a car driver who delivers women to clients is called *mafu* (jockey). Most women from China arrive in Taiwan after "marrying" Taiwanese citizens, who are called *jialaokung* (fake husbands). An agent may also place a Chinese woman in an escort agency or outcall service (often called "company"), with someone like Peter.

Peter, in his thirties, was handsome and friendly. He was very accommodating of my request, arranging an interview with a Chinese sex worker the day I met him. The next night Peter and I arrived at an apartment and went up to a unit on the twelfth floor. A young man and woman were having a good time chatting online with someone in China. Peter introduced us. "This is Mi Mi, and this is Mi Mi's driver—Joe." It was around nine in the evening, and by that time, Mi Mi had already completed seven sessions or "jobs." According to Mi Mi, the last customer she saw paid her for four sessions to please her and to spend a longer time with her, even though he had sex with her only once. One session with Mi Mi cost about $115, and four sessions would have cost that last client $460.

Mi Mi was wearing blue jeans, a black T-shirt, high heels, and a brown leather jacket. She was heavily made up (with green eyelashes), and she had long, black hair. After Peter told her who I was and what I was up to, Mi Mi promptly agreed to be interviewed. Then, one of Peter's four cell phones rang: a client was waiting Mi Mi. Peter said perhaps I could interview her after this session. Soon, the four of us—Peter, Mi Mi, Joe, and me—were in Peter's car heading to an apartment about half an hour's drive away.

Running Around with Mi Mi

The apartment was located inside a huge complex; the man who met us was running a sex venue (called "store") out of rented space there. Peter took a condom out of a box and gave it to Mi Mi before she went upstairs. Peter drove around the complex for a while, just to check for anything unusual. Soon, Mi Mi called Peter on his cell phone, but he did not answer. It was simply a way for Mi Mi to inform Peter that she met the customer and was about to start work. This also meant Peter would start the timing. Normally, one session was forty-five minutes or less. Peter eventually parked the car near the apartment building and turned off the engine, and we waited.

About twenty minutes later, one of Peter's cell phones rang; again, it was a signal from Mi Mi. She had completed her job. Peter moved the car to the front of the apartment and waited for Mi Mi to show up. Joe began to mumble, saying something about how Mi Mi is not a very good "service provider" because she wants to get "things" done quickly. As a result, she was not always popular with her customers. Once Mi Mi was back in the car, she smiled and said, "How's that? Quick enough?" Then she gave Peter $62, which was the money she received from the "store" operator for a session. Mi Mi and Peter had no say in how much the store owner charges a customer; all they know is that they will receive $62 per session.

While we were waiting for Mi Mi, Peter's cell phones were ringing all the time with calls from middlemen asking Peter to deliver sex workers to their clients. Peter would then call his other drivers and order them to take sex workers to various hotels, motels, or apartments. When Mi Mi got back, Peter told her there was another man waiting for her, also in a rented apartment or "store." He told Joe to drive Mi Mi to the waiting client and I went with them, and he got a taxi to another appointment.

By that time, it was around midnight, and Mi Mi was on her way to complete her ninth session. On our way there, even though it was deep into the night and not many people were out on the streets, the police were everywhere. Chinese New Year was around the corner and it was routine for the police to show a strong presence at this time of the year. In some places roadblocks were set up by the police to stop and search certain cars. I was thinking to myself, "This is great, what if we are all arrested and the next day all the newspapers in Taiwan have headlines reporting that a professor from the United States was arrested with a sex worker." Joe, probably sensing what I was thinking, said, "Professor, don't worry. I've been a jockey for many years, I know where to go to avoid being stopped by the police. That's the most basic requirement of a good jockey."

However, when Joe called the "store" operator to say he was on his way with Mi Mi, the operator said the buyer had not arrived yet, and asked Joe to bring her after the buyer got there. So, without much choice, Joe was driving in circles near the operator's place, while Mi Mi, sitting in back, was cursing and saying we should all go home and forget about the whole thing.

Finally, the buyer arrived. Joe pulled up to the entrance of an apartment building and handed Mi Mi a condom as she stepped out of the car. The operator was standing there waiting. Joe mumbled a few words, complaining that it had taken so long for the customer to arrive. The operator just smiled, apologized, and took Mi Mi away.

Going Nonstop

Then followed a very long night. Mi Mi completed this new session, but that was followed by two more sessions with two men who showed up together, the choreography more or less managed by the operator. When Mi Mi called, Joe quickly moved the car to the front of the building. When Mi Mi eventually got back to the car, Joe repeatedly said he was sorry for what had happened, but she appeared to be angry and was complaining unstoppably. She also handed Joe $186. At that point, Mi Mi had completed eleven sessions, and I thought she must be eager to go back to her apartment. However, a few minutes later, Peter called and asked Joe to send Mi Mi to a motel, where a customer had been waiting for a long time. Joe responded by saying, "Mi Mi is already very tired, and if you want her to entertain one more customer, you better talk to her yourself." Joe handed the phone over to Mi Mi. She began to object, and threatened to quit. She also said she did not want to go to that motel because the clients there were often the worst johns. Peter was very patient and persistent over the phone, assuring Mi Mi that this would be her last client for the night. After a while, Mi Mi, probably coming to the conclusion that there was no way for her not to go, said yes.

Around four in the morning, we arrived at a motel for Mi Mi's last appointment. She got out of the car to look for the client's room. Joe and I sat down in a small waiting area. The middle-aged pimp walked in and yelled at Joe because his customer had been waiting for more than two hours. Right at that moment, Peter showed up, and he said hello to the middleman with a grin. The pimp said, "I am not in a good mood now; I don't want to talk." Peter ignored him and just sat down with Joe to go over the day's business. Joe handed over a stash of cash to Peter, and Peter in return gave Joe about $75 as the day's driving fee.

A short time later, Mi Mi returned and said the client was "drunk like dirt" and the session ended very quickly. The customer wasn't even sure whether he had ejaculated, and kept on asking her the question. When Mi Mi told us that, she began to laugh. This day and night, she had had altogether twelve sessions.

From Paucity to Prostitution

Peter dropped Mi Mi in front of her apartment at almost five in the morning. I told Mi Mi that I could interview her the next day, but she said she could do it now. No matter how tired she was, she was in the mood to talk with me. She bought some snacks on the way home, and then she answered my questions while enjoying her food.

> I was born in Yongzhou, Hunan. My parents were farmers, and they had five children. My family was very poor; when I was young, we could not afford cooking oil.
>
> I dropped out of middle school to come out to work, and not long after, I went to Dongguan voluntarily to become a sex worker. I was only eighteen then. After Dongguan, I went to Shenzhen to continue work in the sex trade; I was also once the mistress of a Hong Kong businessman. I went back to my hometown in Hunan in 2003, and after staying there for a while, I went to Shanghai. There, I was able to make only $24 a day as a nightclub hostess; there were simply too many hostesses in Shanghai, too much competition. Since I was not able to make money in Shanghai, I had to find another place to go to.
>
> I went to Hong Kong first, but I was soon arrested and deported back to China. I wasn't arrested in a sex venue; it happened when I was walking down a street. I like Hong Kong a lot, and I hope I will marry someone in Hong Kong one day and move there. I do not like Taiwan, and I am not coming back after this stay.

I came to Taiwan for the first time in June 2005, and I stayed for six months. This is my second visit; I arrived in August 2006. This time, the Taiwanese authorities only gave me a one-month visa, and since I did not apply for an extension, I am out of status now.

When I was living in Guilin, a woman I met there helped me to come here through the use of a fraudulent marriage. That woman arranged for a Taiwanese citizen to come to Guilin to marry me. After the marriage, I arrived in Taiwan with a visitor's visa to see my "husband." She told me very clearly before the trip that I would be working in the sex trade, how much money a customer pays per session, how the money is distributed among all the parties involved, how much I need to pay the jockey and the fake husband, and what kinds of sex services will be provided to our customers. She also stressed that I must provide a type of oral sex called "Fire and Ice in Three Heavens." Ha, ha, ha! I told her I know all these gimmicks; no big deal! After that, I came and it was agreed upon that I would pay $6,250 as the road fee.

Doing Outcalls by "Bus"

At that point, Mi Mi lit a cigarette.

On my first trip here, I first flew to Hong Kong, and then to Taiwan. I went through the immigration checkpoint in Taiwan quite smoothly. It was like the immigration official was asking me questions and answering the questions himself. Whatever he asked me, I just said, "Ah ... ah," and nodded, and then he typed the answers into a computer. The whole process was really funny.

Mi Mi laughed wholeheartedly when she said that.

When I first came here, I worked in a brothel in Changhua (in Central Taiwan). I did not go out at all. At the beginning, there was some business, but it got really bad later. So I was transferred to Taoyuan (about an hour's drive from Taipei), where I began to do outcall. We did not have our own drivers there; we were transported to the customers

in a minivan called "the bus." One advantage of that was we did not
have to pay a jockey fee like we do here in Taichung.[1]

When I arrived here for the second time, I worked at Changhua
before I was recruited by Peter to come to work here. In Changhua, I
personally got only $31 per session. Here, I take in $38 per session; it's
much better. Here in Taichung, we only do outcall; I have my agent, my
agent places me in a "company" [escort agency], I have my own jockey
[driver], and we have to rely on a middleman to refer customers to us.
The owner of this "company"—Peter—answers the phones himself.

For every session, the "company" actually takes in $62, and I get $38
out of that. The rest of the money is split by the "company" and my
agent. I don't think it's fair for my agent to take $12 per session.

I already repaid the $6,250 road fee, and that's why when I came here
for the second time, I did not work for a while. The money I made here?
I sent some of it back to China, I spent some here in Taiwan, and I also
lost some of the money playing mahjong.

Peter had already told me that Mi Mi was very much into playing
mahjong, and she had lost quite a bit of money. Sometimes, according to
Peter, Mi Mi would play mahjong all night long and refuse to go to work.

On days I work, I will start around two in the afternoon. It is not easy
to characterize the customers. All I can say is that they are all local
people from different age groups. Some of them are sick; they like to
remove their condoms when I am not paying attention and they want
to ejaculate inside my body.

Afraid of the Cops

I am afraid that I will run into the police while working here. I am also
concerned that I will run into sick customers or very drunk customers.
Even though I have never been arrested in Taiwan, I have often been
stopped and questioned by the police. When I was in Hong Kong, I was
chased by the police when I was just strolling, and then they arrested
and deported me. I was mad as hell. I don't understand why women

from China are so looked down upon when they are out of China. In Hong Kong and Macau, isn't it true that many women from all over the world are working in the sex trade there? How come they are not arrested? After I return to China, I am going to write Hu Jintao [the Chinese president at that time] a letter asking him to pay attention to this problem.

Mi Mi was dead serious when she said that, and she was also angry.

Here in Taiwan, I do not have many leisure activities. I love playing mahjong, so I will occasionally play the game, but the stakes are not that high. After I make enough money here, I would like to go back to China. I am really tired of this type of lifestyle, and this job. After returning to China, if I have the opportunity to go to another country, I will consider going. After all, I do not know what I can do in China.

I really do not like this line of work because it is hard work and it can also damage your body. Customers here can also be quite deviant; perhaps they watch too many X-rated movies. I am doing this just for the money, nothing else. I am from a big family, and my parents were not able to make much money, so, as the eldest child, I have to be the one to take the responsibility.

I checked my watch and saw it was almost six in the morning. I wanted Mi Mi to keep talking, but I was also exhausted. When I said goodbye to Mi Mi, she gave me her cell phone number in China and asked me to call her if and when I would be in Guilin.

A year later, I was in Shenzhen interviewing sex workers there, and Mi Mi came to mind. I gave Mi Mi a call, thinking that maybe we could chat over the phone if she was in Guilin. She answered the phone, and to my surprise, she said she was also in Shenzhen. She also told me she was about to fly to Malaysia the next day with two female friends. I invited her and her friends to come out for a late night snack, and we met at a hot pot restaurant in Xiangxi Village, an area at the heart of downtown Shenzhen where many sex venues, restaurants, and hotels are located.

I learned that Mi Mi was arrested not long after I had met her in Taiwan. She was arrested not because she was working as an escort; it was while she was playing mahjong. Although people in Taiwan are highly unlikely to be arrested for playing mahjong, Mi Mi was because she had overstayed her visa. When I saw Mi Mi again in Shenzhen, I almost could not recognize her because of her casual dress. The only thing that did not change was her chain smoking. She told me she was going to Malaysia to engage in sex work so that she could make enough money for her to pay her way to Australia, also to work in the sex trade there.

Six Trips to Taiwan in Ten Years

ANGIE IN TAIWAN

Date: June 11, 2008
Place: A hotel in Fuzhou, China
Name: Angie
Age: 32
Marital Status: Single

Born in Yuncheng, Shanxi. Arrived in Taiwan for the first time in 1997, entered another five times over the next ten years. First four trips, flew to Taiwan as "spouse" of a Taiwanese citizen; smuggled into Taiwan by boat the last two trips. At time of interview, had just been deported back to China.

"I prefer working in a sauna because it is straightforward. Both parties know what they are up to."

~~~

Meeting Angie in Fuzhou

Yang Ling, a sex worker I had interviewed in Taiwan, suggested I talk to Angie, who had also worked in Taiwan, so in June 2008 when I was in Fuzhou interviewing Chinese officials for this project, I contacted Angie and met her in the lobby of the hotel where I was staying. She was thin and seemed tired, but greeted me with a warm smile. Because she was referred to me by one her friends, plus Fuzhou was considered her territory, I did not worry that she would be afraid to talk to me in my room. After we arrived in my room, I invited her to sit on the sofa and pulled up a chair. She began to tell me her story.

I was born in 1977 in a remote area near Yuncheng, Shanxi. My parents were farmers and sold their vegetables in a nearby market. I have two sisters and one brother. When I was a child, we lived a bitter life. How much money can you make selling vegetables?

After graduating from high school, I found a job as a waitress in a nightclub in Xian. My salary was about $36 a month. When I saw a hostess receive a $12 tip for just sitting table, I was shocked. I learned that some kinds of money were really easy to earn.

Getting Played

At that point, I met a man. Eventually, he forced me to have sex with him. I was reluctant, but he was persistent. It felt like he had raped me. After that, I thought that he was going to be my husband someday. People from my hometown are very conservative; they believe that if a woman has sex with a man, she must marry him; otherwise, she is not going to have a successful marriage in the future. I was dismayed when this man left me three months later. I learned the hard way that he was just playing with a naïve young woman; he did not really love me. That experience hurt me a lot, and from that day forward I began to view sex in a very different way.

Angie smiled, as if remembering a dramatic turn in her life.

Not long after that man left me, I went to another nightclub to work as a hostess. At first I was only sitting table, because, in my view, sitting table as a hostess was nothing. Going out with customers was a different story. Nevertheless, I did go out with customers once in a while, but I did not sell sex. As a hostess, I made only about $360 a month; I received $12 per table.

Going to Taiwan for the First Time

I met a woman who had just gotten back from Taiwan; I let her stay in my place temporarily. She said it was very easy to make money in Taiwan, and I was so impressed I asked her to help me get there. That was 1997, and then it was not difficult to travel there. A Taiwanese man came to China to marry me; he was nice, and more than twenty years older. We had to travel back to my hometown from Xian to get married because according to Chinese law, the marriage had to be held in either the bride's or the groom's hometown.

After Taiwan and China lifted the travel ban between them in the late 1980s, people across the Taiwan Strait began to marry one another. Many of these were legitimate marriages. However, many of these cross-strait marriages were also fraudulent, as they became a means for sex ring operators to transport women from China to Taiwan for commercial sex.

A month after marrying the Taiwanese man, I went to Taiwan to visit my "husband." I flew to Shenzhen first, crossed the Louhu Checkpoint into Hong Kong, then flew to Taiwan. The woman who helped me make the connection had a boyfriend in Taiwan; he became my agent. Even though he did not have the money to support my trip, he had a money man behind him.

It is no surprise that someone who had no money could still be an agent in this business. All he or she had to do is find a money man or an investor. In the sex trade, I have learned that people from all walks can come together to make money in a concerted effort.

I began to work in Taichung. I was mainly seeing customers in two apartments [or "stores"], even though I occasionally also did outcall. When I first got there, my agent and the investor both thought I was very "country," so they bought me new clothes, got me a new hairstyle, and I became a completely different woman. Even so, they were convinced that I wasn't pretty enough and would not make a lot of money. Later on, I made so much money for them that they realized they were dead wrong about me! That's because I never complained, I entertained as many customers as possible, day in and day out, and I never took a day off simply because I was not feeling well. Even on a day when I had to work until six or seven in the morning, I would get up at two in the afternoon ready to go to work. When I was working, I never rushed my customers, and I took time to chat with them.

Angie looked like she was quite proud of what she was able to accomplish in Taiwan. In her view, she worked hard, fulfilled her duties, and helped her agent and investor earn a lot of money, so there was nothing to be ashamed of in being a sex worker.

Before I left for Taiwan, I was told that I owed them (the agent and the investor) $7,500. I believe they did not overcharge me for the trip; it cost a lot of money to send someone to China and marry me there. My only disappointment was they told me there would be plenty of clients to see in Taiwan and when I got there, there weren't as many as they said.

My other disappointment was that I made only $37 per session. The "store" operator charged a customer $130 to $145 and gave my escort agency $88. Of the $88 the escort agency received from the operator, my agent got $17, my investor took $17, my escort agency received $17, and I got $37. I should have been given $41 to $47; I wasn't aware of how much I should get, and since it was all agreed upon beforehand, I went along.

I stayed for six months on my first trip to Taiwan, and flew back to China on my own without any problems. I repaid my road fee ($7,500) in about two months. It took that long because business was slow at the beginning, plus my monthly fixed expenses were about $3,700, including $74 a day for my jockey, $880 for my "husband fee," $176 a month for rent, money for meals everyday, and money to buy clothes. Every month I was doing my first 100 sessions without making any money [100 x $37 = $3,700]. After staying for six months during my first trip to Taiwan, I made about $12,500 after repaying the road fee. But in China, how the hell was I going to make this kind of money in six months?

Angie was right; not many people can make $12,500 in six months in China. But to make this kind of money, one has to see many clients.

Going to Taiwan for the Second, Third, and Fourth Times

After returning to China for two months, I wanted to go to Taiwan again. However, I learned that my "husband" was arrested by the authorities for bringing white powder [heroin] into Taiwan. After he began to play the role of fake husband, some people asked him to carry a bag of stuff when he was about to fly to Taiwan from China. He was surprised that it was white powder. After his arrest, I told my agent I would pay for his lawyer's fee; he could use the $5,880 I left with him. That meant I would pay a lump sum amount for the husband fee and didn't have to pay $880 per month anymore. And even though he was in jail, his daughter could still sponsor my return to Taiwan.

When I went to Taiwan for the second time, I did not have to pay another $7,500 as road fee but still had to pay a cut of my earnings to my agent and escort agency, and pretty much obtained all the necessary travel documents on my own. Too bad I was arrested three months after I got there. After a few days in a police station, I flew back to China. On my second trip, I was paid $54 per session instead of $37 doing outcall, and that's because I did not need to pay $17 to the investor anymore [only $17 to the agent and $17 to the company or escort agency owner].

When I was in Taiwan the second time, I was extorted by the police. They set up a trap to get me, and after I was arrested for selling sex, they demanded $1,760 for my release. My agent and I came up with $880 each; we were willing to comply because as long as you are free, you don't have to worry about not making money.

After I was deported back to China, I was desperate to go to Taiwan again, though I needed a new and different household registration and then another "husband." Soon, my agent in Taiwan was able to find someone in Hunan Province who was willing to sell her household registration. Then I married a Taiwanese man again. When I went to Taiwan for the third time, my road fee was $6,250. Unfortunately, I was arrested again after three months. I was sent back to China again.

At this point, Angie burst out, saying, "You do not recognize me, do you? We met in Taiwan before! I think once when I was waiting for a customer in a "store," you, Yang Ling, and an escort agency owner showed up." At first I thought, "Oh my God, how can I not remember her!" But then I remembered a woman I met in a "store" in Taichung. At that time, she was wearing a very short skirt, a tight T-shirt, and heavy makeup, and a cigarette dangled from her mouth. Now I understood why Angie was so friendly when I met her at the lobby; I was not a complete stranger to her, after all. After this exchange, Angie became more animated when she talked, as if she was ready to tell me everything about herself and her experiences in Taiwan.

> After I came back to China, I found another woman in Guangxi who was willing to sell me her ID. Of course, I got married again with a Taiwanese man and then made my way to Taiwan for the fourth time. This time, it was worse; I got arrested after two months. At that time, the Taiwanese police were cracking down on sex work involving women from China because there were so many of them. If you were working, there was always the possibility of getting caught anytime. That was 1999.

Going to Taiwan for the Fifth and Sixth Times

> When I came back after my fourth trip, I did not return to Xian but went straight to Fuzhou from the Hong Kong airport. I was upset that I got arrested after only two months in Taiwan. Someone told me I can go to Taiwan by boat, all I needed to do was to go to Fuzhou and take a boat from Pingtan to Taiwan.[1] The cost was about the same as the air route through fraudulent marriage: $6,250. Besides, after the fourth trip, it was not possible for me to go to Taiwan as a "spouse" of a Taiwanese citizen anymore because the Taiwanese authorities began to use fingerprints to identify a person and I can't utilize another person's ID again.

It sounded incredible: a young woman on her way back to the same country that deported her only hours ago. I was wondering what the force was behind this course of action.

> On my fifth trip, I was arrested after working for six months. Because I was smuggled into Taiwan by boat, the Taiwanese authorities would send me back to China by boat. Before that though, I was locked up in a police station for two months, simply because the detention center in

Shinju was so crowded that it had no beds. After I was transferred to the detention center, I spent another seven months there. That was 2003.

The detention center Angie was talking about is called the Jinlu Detention Center, a place where most illegal immigrants from China are kept. I visited the center in 2004, and I saw more than a thousand young women there. I also saw quite a few pregnant women and new mothers at the center waiting to be deported.

After that, we were sent to Maju [a small island under the control of Taiwan but very close to mainland China] and then waited for two more months there. Altogether I was detained for twelve months before they sent me back to Fuzhou. I was locked up for a few days in Fuzhou, and after paying a fine of $600, I was released.

Working at a Sauna in Fuzhou

After my return to China, I began to work in a sauna in Fuzhou. When I came back to China from my first four trips, I did not work at all. However, this time I was in need of money, so I went to work. I prefer working in a sauna because it is straightforward; both parties know what they are up to. In a nightclub, however, it is a different story. There is a lot of fondling; a customer might want to have sex with a woman but doesn't know how to ask for it. Some customers want to go to bed with a woman for free. Also, we have to drink a lot, and wear pretty clothes and heavy makeup.

I asked Angie about her relationships with the many agents in Taiwan and she was very candid about it.

Even though I had been to Taiwan six times, I only worked for two agents, not counting the two agents I worked for for a few days on my fifth trip. I worked for one agent my first three trips, and another the last three trips. I did sleep with the first agent, even though he had a girlfriend; it was nothing. The second agent was in his forties, married, with children, and my relationship with him was complicated; he was my friend, lover, and agent at the same time. That agent was very good at dealing with us; there were four of us working for him, and he was very nice to us. He also maintained a sexual relationship with all of us, and that was how he established an emotional connection with us. Besides, he paid us promptly, and he never took advantage of us financially.

Men Come to Us for the Feeling

I asked Angie how her relationship was with her customers. Did her customers abuse her? Use violence against her?

When we are with our clients, it is more likely that we mistreat our clients, not that our clients mistreat us. What can they do against us? The worst they can do is to rape us! Once we walk into a room with them, they've got to pay us, no matter whether they are pleased or not. If we are in a good mood, we can let them "fly;" otherwise, if we act like we are "dying" and have no response to whatever a client does, how can he be "happy"? If we are in a good mood we will cooperate, we will act, and let a client feel like he is making love with his girlfriend, even though it is nothing but an illusion.

Our mood pretty much hinges on our business. When business is good, our mood is good and we work hard. When business is slow, we will be in a bad mood and we will not work hard. If a customer is not happy with me, I just get up, get dressed, and walk out of the door, what can he do? The customer knows that my driver is going to call me in forty-five minutes, and if I do not answer, he will know that there is a problem.

Even though I am not that pretty, I've had many repeat customers because I know what men want. If I am in a good mood, I can make a man feel very good, like he is in heaven and all of a sudden free of any bondage. I will create a wonderful atmosphere, and he will go home after the first encounter and think of me all the time. That's why my business is often quite good; men come to us for the feeling.

After I got back to China from Taiwan, I met a man who was eight years younger than me. He was one of my customers, and he owns a legitimate business. He went to Xiamen yesterday to take care of some business. My friends urged me to get rid of him, but he said he wants to marry me, so I am not sure what to do. I am now staying at a friend's place, but I can't do this for long, so when my boyfriend is back, we will think about renting a place. I also might go back to Nanchang to work, or Shenzhen—but not Xian.

I've saved less than $4,000. I have not saved much money, even though I've been in the sex trade for more than ten years and have earned a lot of money. I do not know how to save. My family has never asked me for money.

Angie seemed lost after returning to Fuzhou, not knowing what to do with her future. After working for more than ten years, being smuggled into Taiwan so many times, and seeing probably thousands of clients, Angie had not much to show for it.

My plan is to get married after working for two more years; by then I will be thirty-five. However, women like me are not going to get married easily. Most of the men we know are our clients. If we go back to our hometown to find someone to marry, it won't be easy for us to get along with men who have never been outside of their rural area. I also want to go overseas again, like Australia or Dubai, but not Taiwan, because if I get caught again in Taiwan, I will be prosecuted, jailed, and then after being deported back to China, I will be sent to a labor camp. That's a huge risk—not worth it, unless if there is another way to go to Taiwan besides taking a boat.

When we were about to complete the interview, the sky got dark and heavy rain came down like it was going to wash the whole Fuzhou City clean. When I handed her the interview fee, she said, "No, you do not need to pay me." But when I insisted, she took the money and thanked me profusely for it.

CHAPTER 7

Earning Tips in a Flower Hall

MOLLY IN THAILAND

Date: January 29, 2007
Place: Hotel lobby bar in Chinatown, Bangkok
Name: Molly
Age: 26
Marital Status: Married, with a baby son

Born in Songji, Hubei. Graduated from middle school. Several months after giving birth, traveled to Bangkok with her husband's older sister to engage in sex work. Never worked in the sex trade before arriving in Bangkok. This was her second trip to Thailand; working in a flower hall, also goes out with customers.

"After sex, some clients ask me whether women like me still have any real feelings."

~~~

Interviewing Sex Workers in Bangkok's Chinatown

I had been in Bangkok two years prior to this trip and had seen many Chinese women in the adult entertainment centers in the city's Chinatown, called Yaowarat. But this time in Bangkok, I had to rely on a guide (an old friend from high school) to locate a possible interview subject. In the lobby bar of my hotel, my friend introduced me to a woman named Molly, and left.

Molly wore a low-neck black T-shirt, long white pants, and very little makeup. We sat down at a corner table. After we ordered our drinks, I explained to her what my research project was all about. It was around three in the afternoon, and there were no other customers in the bar. Through the large glass windows, we could see the sun was shining, and there were many pedestrians and cars in front of the hotel. Molly began to tell me her story.

I was born in Songji, Hubei. Songji belongs to the city of Jingzhou. I am twenty-six now, married, and have a son. He is only eight months old. My parents are both farmers, I have a little brother who is studying in Beijing now. My parents believe sons are much more important than daughters, so they asked me to quit school after I finished middle school, just to save the money for my little brother's education.

Molly was calm, and did not seem to be bothered by this experience. At this point, our waitress brought us our drinks. She was wearing a traditional Thai dress and knelt down when she placed our drinks on the coffee table. We paused for a moment and after the waitress left, Molly took a sip of her lemonade and continued.

After I graduated from middle school, I studied tailoring for three years and then went to Shenzhen to become an apprentice. A year later, I left to work as an independent tailor, but business was not good. Later, I returned home. At that point, my mom introduced me to a man, and urged me to marry him. I did not take her advice; instead, I married someone else—my current husband. That was a mistake; I married him simply because he once did a big favor for me. I soon regretted the marriage. He was an honest person, but did not know how to make money. I was making about $150 a month then, so it was not enough.

My sister-in-law had been to Bangkok, and my aunt too. After my sister-in-law came back, she told me it was easy to make money in Bangkok, so when my aunt came back, I decided to go to Bangkok with her on her next trip.

Many Chinese women in Bangkok were, like Molly, brought there by friends and relatives from the same hometown. In some rural areas of China, several networks had been established to help women go overseas together so that they could help each other after arriving in a foreign land.

Once I decided to go to Thailand with my aunt, I asked someone to help me obtain my passport, visa, and air ticket. It all cost about $500. I arrived in Thailand for the first time on June 3, 2006; it was also my first trip on a plane. This is my second trip to this country.

Tricked by Her Sister-in-Law

I came here the first time with a tourist visa, returned to China after five months, stayed home for two months, then came back to Thailand on a business visa. Before my first trip here, I had given birth to a baby boy, and I was still wearing a copper T to prevent me from getting pregnant. That trip, I came here with my aunt; she had been in Bangkok for about three years then. We took a thirteen-hour train ride from Hubei to Guangzhou and then flew to Bangkok. Flying to Bangkok was fine; but that long train ride to Guangzhou was exhausting. I had never been a sex worker in China. My sister-in-law did not tell me about going out with men before I left China. I assumed that I would accompany men to drink and sing. I felt like I was tricked into this by her because she did not tell me about sleeping with men.

Was Molly really unaware of the need to sleep with men? Most women I interviewed told me they knew they would have to have sex with men if they worked as hostesses in nightclubs or KTVs. They knew that hostessing was not just about sitting tables.

The first night I arrived in Bangkok, a man met us at the airport and drove us to my aunt's apartment. Then my aunt gave me her cell phone and told me to go downstairs and stay there until she called me. About half an hour later, she called me upstairs. By then, that man [the driver] was wearing only underwear and was walking around the room. I knew right then what they had been doing. After the man left, my aunt told me not to make a big deal out of it and that I will understand it better in a few days. At that point, I did not know what she was talking about. Two days later, my aunt told a man that I just got here and asked if he wanted me to keep him company. My aunt and he agreed that he would pay me about $1,000 if I stayed with him for two weeks. I refused. My aunt said, "Why are you here in Thailand if you don't want to do this? If you do this, you will earn back all your expenses and you won't have to worry about going back to China with a loss." So I packed my things and went with the man to his place.

When I arrived in Thailand there was a little bit of bleeding because of the copper T. After I got to his place, we did not have sex because of the bleeding. He was very nice to me; every day he took me out for dinner and we went to a few places for fun. He waited patiently for me to get well. After nine days, he could not wait anymore, plus he noticed that I was not happy; when I called home, I was crying all the time. Finally, he drove me back to my aunt, and paid me about $500 for those nine days.

Molly's First Client

Now I know why cousins and aunties are willing to bring their sisters and nieces along when they go overseas. First, they can refer them to the highest bidder and make a commission, and second, anyone who is interested in getting close to their sisters and nieces has to be nice to them, too.

It took another two weeks for my aunt to find another man for me; that way she can receive a referral fee from the customer. Eventually, a client took me to a hotel one day. I was nervous, and after I got undressed and he saw how thin I was, he said he couldn't do it, gave me $25 and asked me to leave. I got dressed and started out the door, but he brought me back inside and then we had sex. When I left, he gave me another $105. When I returned to my aunt, she said it was a very good price ($130), but she did not know how much I cried before I entered her apartment.

Molly was a bit ashamed when she said that.

I was already working in a flower hall before that incident. On my first day, because I was new and young, many customers gave me tips. I went home with more than $50 and I was very happy because I did not have to sleep with men to make those tips.

Flower Halls in Thailand

Flower halls are similar to nightclubs or KTVs where young women will act as hostesses in accompanying their clients to eat, drink, and sing. The uniqueness of flower halls is that a hostess receives tips by way of singing on a stage. A hostess must first ask her client to let her go on stage to sing, and while she is singing, the client will ask a waiter or waitress to go up to the stage and hang a ring of plastic flowers on the hostess's neck. The hostess will then publicly thank her client for offering her "flower money." When the client pays the bill, the "flower money" will also be included. There is no money exchanged between the client and the hostess. Some flower halls are decorated like upscale nightclubs, and some are just ordinary restaurants equipped with a small podium for singing.

Everyday, I will rotate among a few buildings in this area around noon, eating with clients to earn tips. Around nine in the evening, I will go to work in a flower hall, and I will mainly sit table, but when there is an opportunity to go out with customers, I will do so.

The flower hall has several private rooms and a big hall, and it is up to the customers to decide where they want to have fun. If a customer wants to offer a hostess a lot of "flower money," it is better doing it in front of a large number of people; in the private rooms, there's more privacy, and this means a customer can have some intimate interactions with his hostess. Most customers prefer sitting in the big hall. There, a customer can offer $6, $9, $15, or $30 "flower money;" some customers pay much more. The flower hall takes $.60 of every $3 in tips, plus the hostess needs to pay a $1.20 protection fee each day. This is applicable to the big hall. If a customer selects a private room, it costs him $3 per hour for the hostess, and $5 for the house. If a customer wants to take the hostess out of the premises for special service, he talks to the hostess and the mommy and they come up with a price. It costs at least $85 to take a hostess out. The mommy will get a percentage from the hostess and a large tip from the client.

I normally go out with a customer once a week—about four times a month. It is rare that I go out twice a week. My clients at the restaurants or flower halls are mainly Chinese-Thai, or Chinese from China. We try not to go out with Chaozhou men because they are regular customers who all belong to a close network, and they would tell everybody they had sex with one of us.[1] So, we only drink tea and sing with them.

Molly was very specific about the inner workings of the flower halls in Bangkok. One of the buildings Molly was talking about is located in the heart of Bangkok's Chinatown, and has about twelve stories. The building is actually a large parking garage, with many restaurants, legitimate massage outlets, and small flower halls located on the second floor. Inside the building, there are many Chinese women wandering around, eating and drinking tea with local elderly Chinese men for tips. Most the men are retired Chinese Thai of Chaozhou origin, and they are there to eat and drink tea, and also to mingle with the Chinese women.

In general, most of my clients are fine; they will buy you anything you want to eat, and I have not encountered any weird men so far. I also had some very happy moments in Thailand. A few days ago, I took a friend from my hometown to meet someone. He was not satisfied with my friend, however. I suggested someone else, but he said that I need not refer anyone to him anymore because he had found what he wants. It was me. He asked to come back to my place. Eventually, I took him home. We talked for three hours at my place and then had sex. I completely forgot that he was my client, even though he paid me afterward. The next night, he came to my home with grapes that I like. We talked and then had sex. He went to Guangzhou on the third day and will not be back for one month. His wife is in Guangzhou. I miss him badly. I have an emotional attachment to him. This is the happiest event I have had in Thailand.

Molly appeared to be quite happy, and she was smiling broadly.

When I returned home after my first trip here, my husband suspected that I had been working in the sex trade in Thailand, but I denied it. I asked him, if I were to remain in China, how would we survive? He knew he did not have the ability to bring money home.

Counting Money Makes Me Feel Real

My mom knew what I was doing in Thailand, and didn't want me to go back there. But I asked her, "What can I do if I stay in China? I get nervous whenever we need money; in Thailand, whenever I go home and count my money, I feel real. I can make at least $400 a month in Thailand." She did not stop me; she just told me to pay attention to my health, and if I am not making it in Thailand, just come home to China. My little brother also guessed what I did for a living in Thailand, but he did not say anything. He told me to take of myself and not work too hard.

Molly's voice was fading when she said this, as if she was talking to herself. For many women, preventing their families from finding out what they were doing overseas was very important. And if their families somehow knew the truth, then convincing them that the sex work was necessary was also a challenge.

In China, I have to spend money every day; here in Thailand, I can make money every day. For me now, the only important thing is how much money I can make. As long as I have money, I am happy. The sex business is everywhere here, and it is a very open society, so I don't worry about being a sex worker here. I have been arrested several times, though, but each time released quickly.

The pianist working for the bar showed up and began to play and sing. It was a pleasant surprise to hear him (a Thai) sing a Chinese song. I asked Molly if she had encountered any trafficked victims in Bangkok.

I don't think you will find any trafficked persons here. Some women arrive after being charged too much—that's possible. Some women were told they would be making tons of money in Thailand, and that was all exaggerated.

What we are doing is an exchange; we offer our bodies for the money we want. There is also no turning back in this occupation. Once you are in, it is not easy to go back to working for $150 a month. For sure, this is also a very degenerate job and it will cast a shadow over my life forever. After sex, some clients ask me whether women like me still have any real feelings. They wonder whether everything for us is just a matter of exchange between money and flesh. Whenever a customer asks me this question, it hurts me.

Molly was trying not to cry when she said that, and her mood was completely different from how it had been when she was talking about the man she recently met. Many sex workers have told me that some customers will say something disparaging and that the harm these words inflict is worse than being hit in the face.

To tell you the truth, I am easily satisfied. I am not greedy, and so far I have never let any men *bao* [to cover or to pack, meaning to have a woman as a mistress] me. There were men who wanted me to be their mistress, but I didn't want to treat anybody like an emperor or act like a slave. I would rather make less money but enjoy the freedom and not be dictated to by one man.

I am twenty-six now, and I can work for at least ten more years. I want to save some money, and have my son go to college. I also want to build a house for myself, and have savings for the rest of my life. That's all I want.

When Molly was almost over with her story, a few customers walked in. The pianist began to sing some English songs. Molly and I sat there in silence for a moment, drinking and listening to the music.

CHAPTER 8

Selling Sex because of Her Brother

TINA IN THAILAND

Date: August 4, 2007
Place: Hotel lobby bar in Chinatown, Bangkok
Name: Tina
Age: 24
Marital Status: Divorced, with a five-year-old girl

Born in a rural area about two hours' drive from Harbin, Heilongjiang. Elder brother's involvement in an assault case put family in deep financial trouble. Out of desperation, came to Bangkok to sell sex, which caused breakup with husband.

"I really regret entering this occupation. If not for my brother, I wouldn't be here."

∽

Brother Got into Trouble, Sister Paid the Price

I stayed in Bangkok for a couple of weeks in January 2007 and conducted several interviews with Chinese women working in the sex industry (mostly in flower halls). Since I needed more interviews, I returned in August 2007. After a day or two of inquiry, I located a woman who worked at a KTV and was willing to talk to me. I interviewed her in the same hotel bar where I interviewed Molly.

The young woman introduced herself as Tina. She was wearing a white T-shirt and white long pants. She ordered a glass of watermelon juice and I asked for a glass of orange juice. After I explained to her who I was and what my research project was all about, Tina began to describe her past.

> I was born in a rural area about a two-hour drive away from Harbin [the capital of Heilongjiang Province]. When I was five, my family moved to Harbin. My father was a truck driver and my mother did not work. She stayed home and was a housewife. I had an elder brother. As far as I can remember, we were doing fine financially when I was young.

When a waitress brought us our drinks, Tina stopped talking and waited while the waitress quietly placed our drinks on the coffee table.

> I quit middle school and started working at a store selling clothes. My base monthly salary was about $60, but with the sales commission, I made about $120 a month. I met my husband when I was working there. We got married and I stopped working. I was nineteen.
>
> Some time later, my brother got in a fight and knifed the other guy. We had to hire a lawyer to defend him, and pay the medical expenses of the wounded man; we also had to bribe the authorities to get my brother a lighter sentence. My family spent more than $12,000 to deal with this incident. Even so, my brother received a three-and-a-half-year prison term. At that point, my father called me and asked if my parents-in-law could lend him $6,000. When I told my mother-in-law about my father's request, she seemed indifferent and unwilling to help. I could not swallow an insult like this, so I decided to come out and earn money to help my family go through this difficult time.
>
> Right at that time, I met a woman from Harbin who was just back from Thailand. She told me how easy it was to make money there. Women working there rely on sitting table to make money, not sleeping with men. I applied for a passport myself, and she helped me get the visa and the ticket. It took only a few days to get my visa. I agreed to pay that woman $1,500. She said she would make sure someone would meet me

at the Bangkok airport and someone else would take me to the place where I would work.

From Harbin to Bangkok

I arrived here for the first time in November 2004 on a tourist visa and stayed for seven months. This is my sixth trip here. On my first trip, I took a bus from Harbin to Shenyang—a seven-hour ride. Another bus from Shenyang to Beijing—a twelve-hour ride. From Beijing, I flew direct to Bangkok. There were five of us. We did not know each other. We were all helped by that same woman from Harbin.

Three Chinese men walked in and took a table not far from us. That caused Tina to lower her voice somewhat.

In Bangkok, a friend of that Harbin woman picked us up at the airport. Three days later, that same woman who met us at the airport took us to work at a flower hall in Bangkok's Chinatown. We were shocked to see how shabby the place was and how old the customers were. But now that we were here, we might as well work and try to make some money to cover our costs before we go home. I did not go out with clients, just sat their tables. Two months later, someone took us to a KTV to work and our mood changed for the better. I also began to go out with clients there.

When I was in Bangkok, I often wandered around the area where that flower hall was located, and I saw many Thai-Chinese men there also. Some of the men were toothless and bald and walked around in sandals and shorts with cigarettes dangling from their mouths. The flower hall was actually just an ordinary restaurant with a toilet that was smelly and dirty. No wonder when Tina walked into that flower hall for the first time, she could not believe her eyes.

Tina told me in further detail how much a client has to pay a woman for drinking with him and sleeping with him. She had become very familiar with all this because she had been to Thailand many times over the past four years and had stayed for a lengthy period on each visit.

This place I am working now is a KTV and it does not have a big lounge—only private rooms. When customers arrive, mommies bring the hostesses out for customers to choose. Each hour lasts forty minutes and it costs $8 per hour. The hostesses get about $3 per hour. Before customers leave, they must also pay at least $15 in tips per hostess. For going out with a client, the client must buy ten hours (pay the house $80) and pay the hostess $140 (but sometimes as high as $285 or $570). The hostess must pay the mommy $30 afterward.

Many people I interviewed for this project told me that most Chinese women would like to go to the US or Japan if they had a choice; followed by Singapore or Taiwan. Those who did not have access to the above countries would consider going to Hong Kong or Macau, then Indonesia or Malaysia, and finally, Thailand. Thailand is not a popular country because, in general, they make less money there. However, after listening to Tina, I learned that some women did make a substantial amount of money in Thailand. Besides, in Thailand a woman does not need to sleep with as many men to make money as women in other countries do.

When I was working for that flower hall in Chinatown, all the clients were Chinese-Thai of Chaozhou descent. In the KTV where I am now working, the clients are mostly upper-class businessmen. The clients at the flower hall located on the outskirts of Chinatown are less classy than those in the KTV; after all, that is a flower hall. However, the clients there are much better than the clients at the flower hall in the center of Chinatown. These clients, regardless of where we meet them, do not force us to do anything, except that some are rude.

When I asked Tina whether she had ever encountered a bad client, someone did immediately come to mind.

Once, I had a good impression of a client, so when he asked me not to work and stay with him, I did so for almost a month. Unexpectedly, he disappeared after a month and did not pay me a penny. Whenever I think of him, I am furious.

Money and Love

Not long ago a Chaozhou man took me as his mistress and supported me on a regular basis, so I did not work for more than a year. He gave me $1,400 a month and I became idle and bored. I did not like that Chaozhou man. He told me he was in his sixties, but I guessed he must have been in his early seventies. While I was taking his money, I did not work secretly out of principle. I am different from those women who take money from their men and go to work as well.

"Well, what about someone who had made you happy in Thailand?" I asked. Tina told me there was one man—a client.

When I was here last time, I met a man from Beijing who is currently my boyfriend. He is married and works at a shipping company. When I was working at a flower hall on the outskirts of Chinatown, he came in with a group of friends. I was one of their hostesses. While we were together, one of his friends said something that offended me, and I cried. The next day, he and his friend took me to dinner and his friend apologized to me. I had sex with him afterward.

I really like him, although we sex workers know very well that we should not be entangled in a romantic relationship with a client. In the past, when I heard that one of us was falling in love with a customer, I could not understand how that could happen. But now I myself am romantically involved with a customer. I know the two of us do not have a future, but people often have feelings for one another, right? To be honest with you, it does not pay to be with him. He pays me only $700 or $800 a month allowance and I have to spend so much time on him. I believe that he is capable of giving me more money. I do not know how much he really loves me.

At this point, Tina became another person. From the moment I first met her, she had been full of confidence and very cool. Now, she appeared lost and confused. She could not understand why a man who really loved her did not give her more money, especially when the man had the ability to do so.

My attention was turned away when some customers began arriving in the bar, probably tourists from Europe. The pianist who came every day also showed up, this time with a female singer. I asked Tina about her usual routine.

> I get up at noon. Sometimes I stay home and cook; sometimes I go to the building in Chinatown where that flower hall is located and find a restaurant to eat lunch. After that, I go home. Sometimes, around six, my boyfriend from Beijing comes to see me. I rented a room near Suriwong Road for $170 a month. I am living by myself for privacy. My Beijing boyfriend gives me more than $1,500 as money just for rent. I go to work at the KTV around nine thirty in the evening, and go home around one thirty in the morning.

I asked Tina about her concerns working in Thailand. I was thinking to myself that since Thailand has a well-established sex industry, selling sex there must not attract the attention of the police that much. I was wrong.

> My foremost concern here is being arrested. On my way home from work, I will sometimes run into police who want to see my passport. Several weeks ago, the taxi we were taking was stopped by the police. All my coworkers had their passports with them but I only had a copy of my passport because I was afraid that I might get robbed and lose my handbag. The police wouldn't let me go until I paid them $90. I said I can give only $15. They said no. Eventually, I gave them $30. They just want money anyway.

Divorce Was Best

Tina had told me she was once married, so I asked her about the divorce.

> When I left China, I told my husband and family that I was going to the United Arab Emirates. If they knew I was going to Thailand, they would think that I might engage in sex work there. Returning to China from my second overseas trip, I got a divorce. My relationship with my

husband had become cold. When one of us suggested that we should get a divorce, we both agreed that it was for the best.

Tina seemed resigned. Perhaps, as she said, by the time they were about to split, there were no feelings for each other, so there was no pain to speak about.

My brother was released from prison after I returned from Thailand last time. He got married. I paid for all his wedding expenses, for a total of more than $7,600. So far, I have saved almost $25,000, but I dare not spend all the money and buy a house; I am afraid people will wonder what I do to make this much money. I told them I am making dumplings in a restaurant in the United Arab Emirates. I am not going to tell anybody I am in Thailand. In China, everyone knows Thailand is very open when it comes to sex.

I finally asked Tina what her plan was for the future. She shrugged.

I live from day to day. I just want to take good care of my parents, let them live a happy life. I do not care about myself. I really regret entering this occupation. If not for my brother, I wouldn't be here. Whatever I do, I do it for my parents and brother. In fact, when my brother got into trouble with the law, I was already married with a child, so I could have ignored him if I wanted. Look at me now, I lost my own family as a result.

I empathized with her, especially when I heard how she took for granted that it was her responsibility to please her parents and brother. I paid the bill and left the bar with Tina. There were quite a few customers in the lounge by that time, and the female singer was singing "The Way We Were." She was marvelous. Tina said she was going home to change; she had to go to the KTV to work that night.

Doing Outcall in Kuala Lumpur

CHLOE IN MALAYSIA

Date: July 20, 2007
Place: A hotel in Kuala Lumpur
Name: Chloe
Age: 21
Marital Status: Single

Born in Changde, Hunan. Dropped out of middle school. Brought to Haikuo by her boyfriend as a teenager and forced to work in the sex trade. After boyfriend arrested, came to Malaysia. Has been to Malaysia many times.

"If not for the money, who would be willing to enter this line of work? It won't take that long to make you feel disgusted in this profession."

❧

Finding an Escort Agency Owner

Before visiting Malaysia the second time for this project, I attended an international conference at the National University of Singapore and met a participant who was a police officer from Malaysia. When I told him I was going to his country soon to work on a research project, he asked me to call him if I needed any help. Half jokingly, I said, "Do you by any chance know any escort agency owners?" To my surprise, he said he did know one large-scale escort business operator in Kuala Lumpur. Since the police officer would be in Europe by the time I visited Kuala Lumpur, he gave me the cell phone number of someone named Michael and told me to call when I arrived in Kuala Lumpur.

A few weeks later, I checked into a hotel in Kuala Lumpur and immediately called that number. The person who answered the call said he was Michael, that a police officer he knew well had already talked to him about my project, and that he was willing to help. It was decided that I would interview a woman in my hotel.

Interviewing Chloe by a Swimming Pool

One evening, after waiting for some minutes in the lobby, I saw a car approach the entrance to the hotel. A manager at the escort agency had given me the last three digits of the car's license plate number, so I knew this was the car I was waiting for. The car was old, driven by a male, with three young female passengers sitting in the back seat. One of the women got out of the car, greeted me in the lobby, and said her name was Chloe. I brought Chloe to the ninth floor of the hotel, where a swimming pool is located. The hotel had more than twenty stories; and the swimming pool was on the top of an adjacent building. That morning, I had walked around the hotel looking for a quiet place to conduct interviews, and decided that the area by the swimming pool would be the best spot.

Chloe did not have heavy makeup, but she was wearing a tight black T-shirt, hot pants, and wooden high-heeled shoes. On the ninth floor, we walked by a restaurant to get to the swimming pool, and we picked a table near a corner and sat down. We were the only ones by the swimming pool outside the restaurant.

Though Chloe had been told by her employer what this meeting was about, I explained to her who I was and what I was doing. She began to tell me her story.

I was born in a rural area near Changde, Hunan. I have an older sister and a younger brother. My dad was originally a driver, but when I was attending elementary school, he was injured when hit by a car, and he stopped working. After that, our family was in a very bad situation financially, and we were looked down upon because we were poor.

Chloe was shaking her head in dismay, and even though she did not go into detail, it was apparent she was still feeling strongly about that experience.

When I was a child, I liked to study, and my grades were not bad. However, I also liked to have fun. When I was in middle school, one of my female classmates was lured inside a building by a group of bad kids. Later, she came out crying, and even though she did not say that she had been sexually assaulted, my teacher accused me of being the one who ordered those kids to do that. Another teacher accused me of being a pimp. So I dropped out of school.

Brought to Haikou by Her Boyfriend

Chloe said she was innocent, and I was not sure how a teenager could be called a pimp by her teachers.

I did nothing but have fun for two years after quitting middle school. Then I went to work in a factory in Changping, Guangdong. I met my boyfriend there. Later, we moved to Haikou and he forced me to work at a bar lounge. A lot of young women sat in the lounge for customers to choose from, and after being chosen, went into a room to have sex. I gave all the money I made to my boyfriend.

In China, some young women are "brought out" by their "boyfriends" to engage in commercial sex. Chloe did not appear to be very upset when she recalled what happened in Haikou; she just lowered her head and smiled bitterly.

I remember when I saw a client for the first time, my boyfriend taught me how to pretend to be a virgin by stuffing something inside me. Throughout the session, I just closed my eyes, and I knew that red colored liquid would flow out of my body. The client was satisfied, and he gave me $360 as tips. After it was over, my boyfriend took the money away.

Chloe smiled again, and it looked like everything was so vivid to her that she was telling me something that had happened yesterday. At that point, a waiter finally noticed that we were sitting there, so he came over in a hurry and apologized. After we ordered some drinks, we resumed our conversation.

I worked in that bar in Haikuo for six months, and he gave me only $180 to send home and let me go home once. At the very beginning, my relationship with him was just sex, but after I realized that he was not that bad to me, I began to have feelings for him. But later, I called the police and he was arrested and sent to jail. He should be out by now, and I don't want to stay in China because I don't want to run into him.

Around that time, I met a woman who had just come back from Malaysia who told me all the good things about the place. I found an agent in China to help me, but he did not have any connections to people in Malaysia, so he located another agent who did help me. Later, I got rid of that second agent, so now whenever I come here, I only have to pay that first agent $130.

Chloe was talking about agents in China and Malaysia who provide their services for a fee, and these agents are not the same as agents in Taiwan. The latter are more like investors; they invest a sum of money to bring a woman from China to Taiwan and act like the "owner" of the woman.

I applied for a passport myself, and they helped me obtain the visa and the air ticket. I gave my boyfriend in China $600 as a "separation fee," gave $600 each to the two agents, and spent another $600 for visa and air ticket. I arrived in Malaysia for the first time in June 2006 as a tourist. I have been here many times now; I stay only one or two months per visit. Every time I come, the "company" sends someone to the airport to meet me.

Company Life, Company "Light"

Chloe spent about $1,900 to come to Malaysia, and even though it was not a small amount of money for people in China, she knew that she could quickly earn it back as a sex worker in Malaysia .

Before I left China, I already knew which company I would be working for in Malaysia; it is the one that I work for now. I joined another company once, but came back to this company. That company wasn't good to work for. This company is a relatively humane one; if you are not happy, they will try to do something to change your mood; if you don't want to work, they won't force you to.

Judging from Chloe's story, it seemed that there were discrepancies between the reality on the street and what had been depicted in movies or in the media. The majority of the women I interviewed told me that their bosses—if they even had one—rarely forced them to work.

I get up around noon, go to the company and wait for business. Here in Kuala Lumpur, my company will drive us to where customers are—their hotels or their homes. Generally, the company will show a customer two women and ask him to choose one. If he is not satisfied, then the company will show him two more. If there are three or four customers, the company will send about five women to let them choose. I normally work until two to three in the morning; if there is overnight booking, I go back to my place around dawn.

The modus operandi of Chloe's company in Malaysia was very similar to the escort agencies or companies in Taiwan since they both involved the delivering of women to customers by car. However, in Taiwan, only one woman is delivered to a client, and if the client "fires a gun" (rejects the woman), the company will send another for him to consider.

We entertain about five or six clients each day; if business is good, we see more than ten clients a day. There are all kinds of men among our clients. Yesterday, I met a man from Saudi Arabia and we were not able to communicate because of the language. He did not release for a long time, and when I could not stand it anymore, I got up and left. Later, my company gave me $30 for the session; I don't know whether my company received any money from that client or not.

My experience in the field suggested that people in the sex business know how to maintain a good relationship with their female workers to ensure there will be more women coming to work for them in the future. If the first waves of women were not happy with their working arrangements, how would it be possible for them to go home and persuade other women to come?

We do not have to pay our driver any money, nor the housemaid who takes care of us while we are here. She will cook our meals, wash our clothes, and clean our place, but we have to pay $18 a day for rent, and $9 as the "turn on the light" fee. We will not be "shining" without their [the company's] "light" [marketing ability]. If we don't have them, customers are not going to find us.

We must go to the company every day. Customers pay the company at least $60 per session. I get $30 no matter how much the customers pay the company. I keep the tips the clients give me. I make about $4,350 a month.

Many women I interviewed were very generous and kind to their parents and siblings, and Chloe was no exception.

Every month after I am paid, I send all my money to my older sister and let her take care of it. She bought a house after she got married, and I later paid her whole mortgage. When my mom was hospitalized, it was me who paid her huge medical bill.

When I am not working, I sometimes go shopping and eating with my coworkers. Most of the time, I just stay in my place and watch DVDs. I don't smoke, drink, gamble, or do drugs. We are relatively free to move around here; our company won't force us to work, and they really do not restrict our movement that much.

Once I was arrested when I was in a hotel with a customer. I was detained for three days and fined $800. I paid the fine on my own; the company wouldn't pay for us. When I was locked up, several sex workers mistreated me because I am physically smaller. Luckily, a Malaysian-born Chinese woman who was detained just like us protected me. That was a horrible place to be in.

No Man Is Good

When I realized time was running out, I asked Chloe about her plans for the future.

I want to buy my parents a house. It is going to cost more than $20,000. For me, marriage is not a must; no matter what, no man is good, it's better to rely on myself instead of a man.

Even though she was calm when she said this, I sensed that she was in general very unhappy with men. Finally, I asked Chloe how she feels about being a sex worker.

If not for the money, who would be willing to enter this line of work? It won't take that long to make you feel disgusted in this profession. I am sick and tired of being poor and looked down upon by other people, so I must go back with a large amount of money. Now, regardless of how unhappy I am, I will force myself to smile when I meet my clients, and think only about the $30 I am going to get soon.

I accompanied Chloe downstairs to the lobby. The car was waiting, with another young woman inside the car. The driver and the young woman took a long, curious look at me. Once Chloe got in, the car left promptly.

Sex Work in a Food Court

LU LU IN MALAYSIA

Date: July 21, 2007
Place: A coffee shop near Jalan Pasar, Kuala Lumpur
Name: Lu Lu
Age: 39
Marital Status: Divorced, with a daughter attending college

Born in a rural area near Jingzhou, Hubei. Did not finish elementary school. Engaged in farming and factory work before sitting table in Taizhou, Zhejiang. This is her second visit to Malaysia. Solicits business in a food court in Jalan Pasar.

"I was about to quit working at the KTV, but after considering how else I would solve my financial problems if I quit, I decided to stay."

~

Jalan Pasar: Groping a Woman for Cheap

A store owner who heard about my research project suggested that I visit a food court in Jalan Pasar; it would definitely open my eyes. *Jalan* means road, and *pasar*, market. I hopped into a taxi and headed for the food court. The driver, a Chinese-Malay who spoke fluent Chinese, told me more.

> I once knew a Chinese woman who was making a living in Jalan Pasar. She was very good at soliciting business, and made as much as $2,000 a month—an incredible achievement. These women are human beings; if they were not desperate, they would not come to Malaysia and engage in this line of work! These women are discriminated against and getting played here, and it must be tough for them. The bottom line is, Chinese men need to search their souls. Why let their wives go overseas to become sex workers? The women here bring a lot of joy to many people, including those working class men in Jalan Pasar. Where can you find a place like Jalan Pasar in this world? You sit down with a beer and snacks, and a woman will come over right away. You give them $3 and they will let you grope them!

The driver dropped me near a large food court where hundreds of people were milling about, eating, drinking, and talking. All the men appeared to be Chinese-Malay, wearing shorts and sandals, and the women, Chinese. Some of the women were sitting with men; others were wandering around looking for someone to talk to. There were probably more than a hundred small and large tables. The place was extremely crowded. I found a table and ordered a beer and some snacks. Once I sat down, quite a few women came over one after another and asked me whether I needed their companionship. The women appeared to be in their thirties or forties, all dressed in blouses and long pants. At the end of the food court there was a stage where a male singer was singing into a microphone.

The place was packed, and very noisy. The floor was littered with garbage and cigarette butts, the air filled with cigarette smoke and the odor from a toilet. After I finished my beer, I walked outside to catch some fresh air. I was surprised to see a lot of women standing there also. Very soon, a woman came over and asked me whether I would be interested in going to her place to have fun for $30. I finally figured out what was happening: outside, on the sidewalk, business was more direct. In the food court, however, both sides needed to sit down to eat and drink first, and sex follows only if both sides want to go further. If the man is not interested, all he needs to do is offer the woman a tip. Of course, the woman is always entitled to a free meal. I smiled and shook my head, and she walked away. Not far from where I was standing, a man in his fifties was approached by a woman; after a few moments, the two of them left; she walked in front and he followed. Apparently, the two sides had agreed on a price, and he was following her to her place.

Very soon, I became aware of another woman nearby. I looked at her and she looked right back at me. Finally deciding that I should take the initiative, I walked over and started a conversation. I asked her the price, and she said $30. I told her I was willing to pay but was only interested in interviewing her for my project. She nodded her head right away.

We walked over to a nearby hotel and found a coffee shop on the first floor of the hotel. There was only one table occupied by two customers, so it was very quiet. We sat down at a table near the corner, and ordered two glasses of orange juice. I told her who I was and what the nature of my project was. She introduced herself as Lu Lu, and she assured me that she was very much willing to tell me her story.

Entering Sex Work at Age Twenty-Nine

Lu Lu wore a black blouse and black pants. I asked her to tell me her family background first.

I was born in a rural area near Jingzhou, Hubei. My parents were farmers, and I have an elder sister, a younger brother, and a younger sister. My family was very poor when I was young; I began to help my parents harvest the land after I dropped out of elementary school. When I was eighteen, I went to Jingzhou to work in a factory; later, I was involved in the clothing business.

I married when I was twenty. My husband was a gangster. We had a baby girl one year after the marriage. My husband gambled and visited sex venues regularly. One day, my husband demanded that a friend repay his debt, and under pressure the friend killed a taxi driver and took his car. He gave the car to my husband as repayment, but when he was arrested, he told the police that my husband was an accomplice. My husband fled to Haikuo. Later, when I went to Haikuo to find him,

I discovered he was living with another woman. I was heartbroken, but what could I do?

Lu Lu began to weep. I handed her some tissues to wipe away the tears and I also quickly surveyed the surroundings; luckily, no one was paying any attention to us. Lu Lu continued her story.

After I returned home to Jingzhou, I was arrested by the police—they were trying to force my husband to turn himself in. I was locked up for more than a month, then my husband returned home and surrendered. He received a three-and-a-half-year sentence. I was really desperate; I had a daughter to raise, and we owed lawyers and others a lot of money. I had no choice but to go to Taizhou, Zhejiang to be a KTV hostess.[1] I was almost twenty-nine.

On my first day at work at the KTV, a client dragged me into a small room off a private room, removed my underpants, and was about to force me to have sex with him. I cried and cried, and he finally gave up. I was about to quit working at the KTV, but after considering how else I would solve my financial problems, I decided to stay. The client pays the house $12 per hostess, and the hostesses get half of the money. If we run into someone we like, we will also go out with him. At that place, I was able to make at least $725 a month by just sitting table as a hostess.

A Painful Past

It was quiet in the coffee shop, and it seemed like the hotel did not have much business either. Lu Lu continued.

A few years later, I went back home, but things were still bad there. Not long after that, my husband also came home from prison. I returned to Taizhou to work, and my husband continued to sleep with other women. Eventually, I was so upset that I demanded a divorce. He agreed. I had been a very good wife and took very good care of our home. I never thought that our marriage would end up like this. When I was working in Taizhou, I brought home money, and I also gave him some.

Soon, Lu Lu was crying again. It was obvious that even though those incidents occurred many years ago, it was still painful for her to talk about them. I asked her whether she wanted to take a break, but she said no.

> After the divorce, I met a man who was poor, but because he treated me nice, I married him. My ex-husband also tied the knot with another woman, and he took custody of our daughter. She is now a college student in Wuhan; she is in her third year. My second marriage lasted only four years.

Lu Lu's eyes had been filled with tears most of the time since the beginning of the interview; she looked happy only when she was talking about her daughter.

> After working as a hostess for a few years in Taizhou, I was promoted to a manager [or mommy]. Not long after, I met another man who was married. I stopped working as a KTV manager and found a regular job instead, but whenever I needed money, I went back to my KTV manager job. This third man did not have any money either, plus he was a gambler. He gambled away more than $12,000 of my money. He did not take care of his own family either. We are still in touch. I think he is now in Jingzhou, waiting for my return.

It seems many sex workers would stop their engagement in sex work when they meet a man they like, or at least will only sit table and not go out with clients. This is their way of showing loyalty to their men. However, once they are in need of money they quickly return to sex work. Lu Lu cried whenever she mentioned the three men in her life, and she blamed herself for her bad luck. The waiters there finally noticed that Lu Lu was crying, and they began to keep an eye on us from a distance.

Trying Her Luck Abroad

> Last year, I met a woman who said Malaysia was a good place to make money. I was also having a hard time making money as a mommy in the KTV in Taizhou, so I decided to go overseas with her to try my luck.

We came to Malaysia on our own. My friend took the lead; she did not charge me any money. I got my passport, visa, and air ticket on my own. I got my tourist visa in a week. Two other women came along, too. We flew to Kuala Lumpur from Shenzhen and then went to the Genting Highlands because my friend used to work there.

When Lu Lu talked about her trip to Malaysia, she began to lighten up and flashed a smile. For many Chinese women who go overseas for the first time, it must be a moment of great excitement and nervousness. Nowadays, there are so many direct flights from major cities in China to various urban centers in Southeast Asia, and it is relatively easy to travel abroad. These direct flights normally take only a few hours.

Genting Highlands is a casino resort and a major tourist attraction in Southeast Asia. It is located on top of a hill near Kuala Lumpur and is equipped with casinos, restaurants, hotels, nightclubs, and a variety of entertainment centers.

After we checked into a hotel, we went to the casino to look for clients. To avoid attention from the security people, we bought some chips and gambled. However, some of us got caught up in gambling and did not solicit much business. As a result, they did not make much money, and lost it at the gaming tables. So we all went back home. That was in 2006.

When Lu Lu was talking about the women who loved to gamble, she always used the word "they," as if she had nothing to do with gambling. Later, however, she told me she, also, was very fond of gambling.

I took this second trip on July 3, 2007. We also went to the Genting first, but because the business there was slow, we came to Jalan Pasar. We make about the same amount of money in both places, but we have to work harder here than in the Genting. Seeing two clients in the Genting generates the same amount of money as seeing four to five clients here.

Lu Lu told me they came to Jalan Pasar because business was not good at the Genting, but I believe the more probable reason was that the security guards at the Genting were making these women's lives in the casino very difficult. She continued.

My first trip, I spent $500 altogether for passport, visa, and air ticket. Plus, I also brought along $750 so I can show the money to the Malay customs. I saved this money when I was working as a mommy in Taizhou.

Here in Jalan Pasar and in the Genting, we find clients ourselves, so we keep all the money our clients give us. In the Genting, we bring our clients back to our hotel rooms, and here, we take them back to our rented apartments. We do not dare stay in a hotel here because we are afraid that the police might come to check our rooms.

We get $60 per session in the Genting and $30 here. In both places, we make about $130 a day. In the Genting, we can make this kind of money seeing two clients. Besides, the clients there also give us tips, and they are very generous. It is difficult to find clients in the Genting because most men go there to gamble. It's difficult to save there; not only may we lose the money we make, we also may lose the money we brought from China. Moreover, if the hotel staff there suspects we are doing sex work, they stamp a seal on our passports and we can't stay there anymore. But one nice thing: the air there is fresh and the weather is cool; we need to put on long sleeve shirts all the time.

Flesh Court

According to Lu Lu, working conditions in Jalan Pasar were harsh.

> Every day I come to this place around noon to find business and go back around three in the morning. I am afraid of being arrested here, so I am scared sometimes. People told me this food court is like a flesh court; when I heard that, it made me very sad.

Now I knew why the business in this hotel was slow; men who bought sex in this area would not bring a sex worker to this hotel because they were afraid of a police raid. Most women working in Jalan Pasar will bring their client to their apartments because it is more discreet. Finally, I asked Lu Lu what her plans were for the future.

> All I am thinking about is making and saving some money from this trip so I do not have to come back again. I want to see my daughter

graduate from college. Plus, I also would like to find a partner; I am not young anymore.

After the interview, I checked my watch and noticed that the interview with Lu Lu had lasted for more than two hours. Of course, the interview with Lu Lu was interrupted a few times because of her crying, and she was very precise in her description of events. I gave her the interview fee, and after she took the money, she did not seem eager to return to the sidewalk where I met her.

Walking the Streets of Geylang

JESS IN SINGAPORE

Date: January 15, 2007
Place: A small hotel in Geylang, Singapore
Name: Jess
Age: 25
Marital Status: Single

Born in Shenyang, Liaoning. Both parents work for the government. Dropped out of high school. Not happy with salary as secretary, so became a street prostitute in Singapore.

"Some are doing it because they want to live a good life; they want to eat good meals and wear good clothes."

～

Geylang: A Red-Light District in Singapore

Working in the red-light district in Singapore called Geylang are women from China, Thailand, Malaysia, Indonesia, Myanmar, and India, plus a few transvestites from Thailand. In Geylang, there are many places where sex workers can be found: massage parlors, brothels, KTVs, nightclubs, and on the streets. Once I landed in Singapore, a relative who has been living there for many years introduced me to one of his friends, and this friend said he would ask a former gangster called Johnny to help with my fieldwork in Geylang.

My meeting with Johnny in a coffee shop in Geylang had been set up by a friend. Johnny was a stocky, powerfully built fellow with tattoos visible under his T-shirt—a sure sign that he had been a member of a tangpai. In Singapore, organized crime groups are called *tangpai* in Chinese, meaning "party" or "clique."

We started at the intersection of Geylang Road and Lorong (lane) 6 and walked all the way to Lorong 38. On the north side of the road, which stretches for about three kilometers, are odd-numbered lanes; the ones on the south side are even-numbered. Most street prostitutes and indoor sex venues are located on the even-numbered lanes. Chinese women seemed to congregate between Lorong 6 and Lorong 20, though many also were strolling along Geylang Road, or were eating and drinking with Singaporean men inside the teashops that dotted both sides of the road.

Somewhere along Delmar Street we saw about twenty Indonesian women openly soliciting business. They were much more aggressive than the Chinese; trying to strike up—in English—conversations with all the passersby. Johnny told me these Indonesian women charged only $23 per session. I saw some men being coaxed into a small shabby house by these women.

Further along, there was a young Indonesian woman talking with a man in an agitated way. The two of them began yelling at one another, and the woman pushed the man away. I guessed the woman must be a sex worker, and apparently very upset. Then, more than a dozen men rushed in from all directions and began to hit and kick the man; very quickly he fell to the ground. Even so, the men continued their attack, hitting him in the head with a folding chair until his head began to bleed. There were more than a hundred people around, but nobody intervened. After the attackers walked away, the man lay there a long time until two men lifted him back to his feet. Johnny told me the attackers were all jockeys (protectors or pimps) of the Indonesian women, and they do not hesitate to beat anyone who tries to take advantage of the working women there.

Later, Johnny showed me a few upscale Malaysian massage parlors (which charge $66 to $130 per session), several so-called Fish Shops where imported Thai women work (for about $25 per session), a number of multinational brothels, and several massage parlors where the masseuses are all from China. I also saw a group of transvestites soliciting business on one of the streets. At another spot were Indian women in traditional dresses sitting outside small shacks, waiting for customers. We also went to the outskirts of Geylang to take a look at some of the KTVs there. We covered a lot of territory.

Interviewing a Street Walker in Geylang

When we got back to Delmar and Lorong 8, it was about ten in the evening, and the place was even busier than it had been an hour before. I told Johnny I would like to interview one of the Chinese women standing there. He said, "Professor, I will go talk to them. Don't be nervous. If something happens, you just walk away. Don't be concerned about me. I will take care of things myself. In Geylang, the bigger group always beats up the smaller group, so it's not a big deal. If I get beat up today, as long as I am not dead, I will come back tomorrow with a large group to claim back my face." These words from Johnny made me all the more nervous, and I could not help but remember the beating of a man by a group of jockeys only a short time ago.

Soon, Johnny approached a young woman and began to talk to her. She seemed taken aback by Johnny's description of my interest in an interview with her. Just then, a man in his forties showed up, asking what the problem was. He, like Johnny, was wearing a long-sleeved T-shirt, even though the night was hot and humid. (Many gangsters in Singapore began to hide their tattoos after the authorities started to crack down on organized crime a few years earlier). Johnny began to describe my project. Once the jockey heard the words "professor," "research," and "interview," he began to shake his head and wave his hands. He told us, in so many words, to go away.

Undaunted, Johnny walked over to another woman but it was the same scenario: a perplexed sex worker, a hyper-protective jockey. After Johnny's third attempt, I asked him to stop.

A New Strategy

The next day, I returned to Geylang alone, having decided on the strategy of asking for an interview once inside a hotel room. When I was wandering around Lorong 14, I saw three white men talking to a young woman in English, telling her she was beautiful. After the men left, I walked over to the woman and asked her how much she charged, and other typical questions, and soon we reached an agreement.

We walked across the street and entered a small hotel. There were many small hotels in Geylang, and all the Chinese women soliciting business on the streets utilized these hotels to see clients. When we arrived at the hotel counter, I found out that we must register, even though we only asked for a clock room. I reluctantly handed my passport to her, and was more uneasy when she said brightly, "Oh, you are from the United States!" She wrote down my name and passport number in a register book, and after I paid for the room, handed me a key. I also was told that my passport would be returned when I checked out.

We took the elevator to the second floor and looked for the room. The corridor was dim, and we walked by a cleaning lady who gave us a cold stare. Once we entered the room, I asked her to sit down, described my research project, and asked if she was willing to participate. She said yes, without much hesitation.

In Search of a Good Life

After Jess sat down, she began to tell me her story.

> My name is Jess, born in Shenyang, Liaoning.[1] My father works for a state-owned iron mill, and my mother, the railway company. Before completing high school, I left and worked as a secretary in a trading company, making $150 a month. You can't have a good life with only a $150-a-month income. I like eating good meals and wearing good stuff, so my income was absolutely not enough for me.

Jess did not offer any excuse for her engagement in sex work, readily admitting that she was doing it because she wanted the money to live a good life. The room was dark, mainly because the curtains had been pulled down (and it seemed to me had never been rolled up).

> Back in China, I already heard that one can make money in the sex trade in Singapore. I was here three years ago for sightseeing and meeting my relatives here, and I visited Geylang then. A month ago, I decided to come to Geylang to be a streetwalker simply because I cannot stand living on a $150 monthly income.
>
> Coming to Singapore was a simple process. There are so many ads in the newspapers in Shenyang saying they can help you to obtain a visa to go to such and such country. I called one of the ads and set up an appointment to talk about going to Singapore.
>
> At the meeting, we did talk about engaging in sex work in Singapore, about walking the streets of Geylang, and about the road fee. They said they could get me a two-year, multiple entry business visa, costing $3,800 for the trip. In the past, when the sex business in Singapore was very good, it used to cost $6,350 to $7,600; now that business is slower, it only costs $3,800.
>
> I left China a month or so later, and arrived in Singapore via Hong Kong, with four of us leaving from Shenyang. We all were in possession of Chinese passports and two-year Singapore visas.
>
> At the airport in Singapore, two men picked us up and drove us to Geylang. I settled down in a single occupant room that cost $20 a day; some females stay in a multiple occupancy room and it costs them only $7 a day. For meals, we simply eat outside.

"This Apartment Disapproves Hookers from Staying"

I did not know where Jess and other women lived, but I believe it was close to where they worked—Lorong 14. I remembered seeing an apartment building with a huge, eye-catching signboard at the entrance, with the words in Chinese and English: "This residential apartment disapproves hookers from staying here."

> Once I got here, they showed me around Lorong 14, and the next day, I began to work. I made a total of $660 that first day. I felt very good about

that. I simply stood there motionless, waiting for clients to approach. I normally charge my clients $50 per session.

If Jess had been standing motionless that first day, it is likely that she was standing under an umbrella. The sun shines brightly in Singapore during the day time, and many of them carry an umbrella to shield themselves from the sun.

> I did not have to pay any money when I left China. After I got here, they [the sponsors] will take away my money everyday. That is the deal. After working for seven days, I repaid $2,000, and I probably will clear all my debt before I leave. We can only stay for fourteen days; after that, we must go to Malaysia and then return to Singapore, or find a way to get an extension here.

Jess was not very precise on this point, but it was clear that there were people behind the massive arrival of Chinese women in Singapore for prostitution. But what about the assertion by the United Nations or the United States government that many of them were either tricked or forced into prostitution overseas?

> Nobody forced me to come to Singapore to engage in sex work. If that's the case, I can always call the police here. In Singapore, forcing someone into prostitution is a serious crime. I enter this work willingly because I want to make more money. Some females are doing it because they have no choice; they need money to survive or to repay a debt. Some are doing it because they want to live a good life; they want to eat good meals and wear good clothes.

The Clients and the Jockeys

While I was listening to her story, I also kept an ear on what was going on outside the room. I was worried that the police might come, or Jess's jockey come looking for us after he suspected something was fishy. Fortunately, it was quiet outside. Because Jess said she began to see clients only after arriving in Singapore, I asked her how difficult it was for her at the beginning.

> I did not have to do anything to prepare myself to do this. As I said, I began to work the next day after I arrived here. Anyway, I had three boyfriends before, so I had sex before. All they told us is that every lorong is protected by somebody, so we can only walk this lorong and can't go over to other lorongs.
>
> Every lorong belongs to a separate group of people. Some play the role of chickenheads and some are lookouts. They can't be considered an organization. I only had contact with three men and they are all Singaporeans. They treat us all right. They don't take advantage of us because if they did, it wouldn't be easy for them to lead us because we would not follow their orders. These people all have tattoos, but they are not bad to us.
>
> So far, I gave them all the money I have earned here—about $2,000— as a road fee. Every time I pay them, they record the transaction. I also keep a separate record. I never heard about them having any money-related disputes with any women here.

Three Concerns

For the majority of Chinese women working in the overseas sex industry, being arrested is their number one concern, and this is also the case for Jess. That's why every lorong in Geylang is watched by a lookout on each end, just to make sure that there will be no surprise raid by the police. Once a lookout suspects that the police are coming, he will inform the jockeys, and all the women will be ordered to take refuge inside a nearby hotel. Under such circumstances, can we say that these women are being tightly controlled by their facilitators in the sex trade? According to Jess, this is not the reality.

> I am absolutely free. All my travel documents are in my hands. They are not afraid that I will run away. Besides, they know where I live in Shenyang. Neither will I flee just because I owe them $3,800; it is not

that difficult to make that amount of money here. Besides, where could I go in Singapore after I leave them?

There are only three concerns working here: I can't make money when business is slow; I can't walk the streets because of rain; I am afraid of being arrested.

I asked Jess whether she regretted entering prostitution. Her answer appeared to be a paradox.

If I had to start it all over again, I would still come to Singapore to engage in street prostitution because it is easy work and I can make a lot of money. However, if I meet a female who is thinking about doing what I am doing, I will urge her not to follow my steps. Standing by the sidewalk waiting for business is tough, and you feel lousy doing it. The bottom line is, after I became a sex worker, I felt like I was living on the edge, and I looked down on myself.

Our conversation ended when Jess's cell phone rang, and I believe it was from her jockey. She told the caller she just completed her job and was about to come downstairs. I was a little nervous, so I asked her to move fast, and quickly paid her. Back out on the street, Jess went back to the spot where she was standing before we met, so that she could wait for the next client.

A Feminist Hostess

MICHELLE IN SINGAPORE

Date: January 23, 2007
Place: A hotel bar near a nightclub in Singapore
Name: Michelle
Age: 28
Marital Status: Single

Born in Beijing. After graduating from college, worked as an entry-level clerk, but not happy with salary. Went to Hong Kong to work as a nightclub hostess on friend's suggestion. Later, decided to go to Singapore.

"I am a feminist, I can't pretend to be a little bird in need of someone to lean on."

~~~

Upscale Nightclubs in Singapore

While still in Singapore, I thought I should interview hostesses in KTVs and nightclubs, but because of my limited budget, I realized I could not go to these places as a paying customer. Nonetheless, around six o'clock one evening, I went to one of Singapore's best-known nightclubs, thinking that a woman working there or in one of the clubs nearby might be willing to talk to me before she goes to work. Because of a luxury hotel nearby, the area was packed with people and cars. I saw many young women walking by, some talking on their cell phones in Chinese. However, I was not sure how to approach them. I was also concerned about asking a non-hostess woman for an interview about sex work by mistake.

Business seemed to be very good for the hotel and the various nightclubs that night. Luxury cars were coming and going, the parking attendants and hotel employees in uniforms busy greeting and taking care of their customers. More young women began to show up. They were in glamorous and fashionable dresses, and I could smell their perfume as they swept by me.

Many of the women stayed in the apartments nearby and walked to work individually or in groups between six and eight in the evening. They walked across the boulevard first and then along a footpath to arrive at the nightclubs. At the rear of one building there was a statue with four faces, similar to the famous four-faced Brahma statue at Erawan Shrine in downtown Bangkok. The statue seemed very popular with the women in that area; I saw many of them stop by to pray and burn incense.

Some women arrived in luxury cars, mostly shiny black Mercedes, and I guessed that they were dropped off by their regular clients. Men were arriving, too; they were in business suits, though some had removed their neckties, and they were all in a good mood, as if they were ready to have fun. Some of them had probably already eaten their dinner and consumed quite a bit of alcohol, and they were walking erratically. They were all Singaporeans no doubt, because they were speaking English in the uniquely Singaporean style called Singlish. One well-dressed gentleman happily shared his thoughts with a man beside him: "After we get drunk in Singapore tonight, we can do the same tomorrow night when we meet in Shanghai."

Michelle from Beijing

At that point, I saw a Chinese woman, alone, walking towards me. She was in a black dress, had long silken hair, and appeared to be a seasoned worker in the adult entertainment industry. Once she heard that I wanted to chat with her and was willing to pay, her immediate response was "How much?" I just blurted out a figure: "One hundred" (Singaporean dollars; about $70). She nodded her head.

The bar inside the hotel was an ideal place to do an interview. The place was nicely decorated, and with only a few customers, was relatively quiet. We picked a corner table to sit down, and then ordered our drinks. I told her what my project was all about. She listened quietly with a smile, then asked me to pay her first. I reassured Michelle that I would definitely pay her after the interview, and asked her to understand my procedure. She quickly said fine, and we began with the interview.

> I was born in Beijing. I am twenty-eight, single. I graduated from college. My father is a government employee, and my mom a housewife.
>
> After college, I worked as a clerk and made a meager income. I had a friend working in Hong Kong, and when she asked me to join her, I did. I did all the paperwork myself. That friend was in the sex trade, and helped me to begin work in a nightclub. I worked as a hostess, and I also went out with clients.

As a person who had worked as a hostess in Hong Kong, Michelle certainly knew how to engage in a conversation and express herself. When she talked about her work as a hostess in Hong Kong, she sounded like it was just another kind of work, not worth making a big deal over. A middle-aged waiter in a white suit brought us our drinks.

> I came to Singapore for the first time in December 2004, also with the help of my female friend in Hong Kong. I had a tourist visa the first trip, but after that, began to fly back and forth between Hong Kong and Singapore with a two-year business visa for Singapore. Now, I only work in Singapore, because the place, the clients, and the quality of life here are all better. Hong Kong is simply too crowded.
>
> When I came to Singapore, I got all the travel documents myself. I only paid for the passport and visa fee. Only women from the rural areas need help when they go overseas. Those who live in Beijing and Shanghai know how to go abroad on their own. Of course, when I went to Hong Kong, my friend there helped me settle down and find a job in a nightclub; and she also set up the connection for me to come to Singapore.

Sitting Table, Rotating Table, and Leaving Table

After arriving here, I came to work for this nightclub right away. I have been working here for the past two years. I like this place so much. I do not think about working somewhere else. The customers are high class. They are all businessmen. After the customers settle into a room, a mommy will bring in women for them to select to sit their table. During happy hour, we normally will go around to various tables, and receive tips in the amount of $33 per table. In the evenings we may or may not go around to the tables, it depends. In the evenings, we will earn $66 to $100 in tips per table.

If we go out with customers, we get $200, but we need to give $33 to our mommy. If a mommy negotiated a higher price with a client, say $270, then the hostess must give her mommy $70.

The tips for sitting table are given to us directly by our clients, so the house and the mommies will not take a cut. However, we are always under pressure from the mommies to drink as much as possible so that the clients will buy more bottles of alcohol. It costs more than $270 a bottle in our nightclub.

At that point, Michelle stopped and then uttered, "I hope you are not a cop!" She looked a little nervous, probably feeling uneasy about telling a stranger the inner workings of her nightclub. I stopped the interview and reiterated who I was and why I was conducting this project, and I showed her my American passport. Once Michelle was convinced I was not a cop, she resumed her storytelling in earnest and told me in detail about her nightclub.

The hostesses in our nightclub are not divided into groups, and this means all the mommies are in charge of all the hostesses. That nightclub across the boulevard has several groups of hostesses, and each mommy there is assigned to one group of hostesses.

Most of the hostesses in my nightclub are from Shanghai, Sichuan, and Hunan; very few are from Beijing. Beijing women are unlikely to engage in this kind of work. We got many young women in there, more than a hundred, because our boss does not reject anyone from working there. He is not picky, you can work as long as you are willing to pay $14 for a badge. You can come and go whenever you want. Those hostesses who are not pretty enough are going to stop coming to work if they do not have tables to sit [no clients] for a few days.

I can make more than $6,600 a month, but I can't save much because my rent is high and I also spend quite a lot of money on food and shopping. So far, not only can I not effort to buy an apartment here, I could not do so in Beijing either.

Every day, all I do is work, both the early and late shifts. But we are also free; if we are not in a mood to work, we just do not work. Nobody is giving us a salary, anyway.

I have at least one table to host everyday, but of course some days I might end up having no clients at all. It is very rare to have this happen for sure. I can make about $200 a day just being a hostess. Our clients are mostly Singaporean businessmen, so they are well-mannered, and they won't behave recklessly inside the private rooms. In some of the other nightclubs, a client can have sex with a hostess inside a back room. Most of our clients are also married men.

No Gambling, Drugs, or German Shepherd Puppy

Michelle had only good things to say about her clients.

I do not have to do anything to cope with my work here. I do not gamble, use drugs, or own a German shepherd puppy. You know what it means to own a German shepherd puppy, don't you?

Michelle asked me this with a smile. A German shepherd puppy is Chinese slang for gigolo.

For me, to be a sex worker is not a big deal. I entered this line of work for a very simple reason: to make money. I am very independent, I like to rely on myself, and I know I need money to live a comfortable life. Of course, I wouldn't be starving if I stayed in Beijing, it just that I want to make some money when I am young so that I won't have to worry about money when I am old. I never thought about finding a man to support me. That's why my process of entering prostitution was straightforward, and I did not struggle at all in the process. I made up my mind and I did it; going down to the sea is no big deal.

Michelle was talking rapidly, and she was convinced that selling sex was the best option for her. She also asked me a few times why the hell I was studying the sex trade, because, in her opinion, there are so many other problems more worthy of study.

If you ask me what one incident might have had any impact on my decision to enter commercial sex, perhaps the divorce of my parents could be it. I was only fourteen then, and the divorce scarred me forever.

No one forced me to enter the sex trade; that is not possible. To tell you the truth, it is not easy to trick someone. We know what we are doing. Maybe there are some females in Malaysia being tricked or forced, but not in Singapore. This is a very well-managed society, and all the females here are selling sex voluntarily.

I Am a Feminist

Most of the women I interviewed for this project assured me that no sex workers in the country where they were working were trafficked; if there was trafficking, it could only happen somewhere else.

I was in love before, but I can't be with those chauvinistic Beijing men for long. I am a feminist, I can't pretend to be a little bird in need of someone to lean on.

Michelle grinned, and she surely did not look like a little bird. I asked her what her plans were for the future.

I really do not have any plans—just getting by one day at a time. I will continue to work in Singapore and make money, but won't go to other countries. I would like to go to the United States, but my English is not good, plus those who can go to the US are mostly people with power and connections. I also heard that one can make good money in Japan, but I don't speak Japanese.

When she finished talking, I gave her one hundred Singaporean dollars. Once she received the money, she stood up and left. I did not stop her, knowing that she had to go to work.

A One-and-a-Half-Million-Rupiah Spa

COLA IN INDONESIA

Date: January 24, 2007
Place: The lounge area of a spa in Jakarta
Name: Cola
Age: 21
Marital Status: Single

Born in Huaihua, Hunan. Completed middle school. Raped at age fourteen, later brought to Changde to engage in commercial sex. This is her first trip to Indonesia. Working in a spa.

"The man who brought me into the sex trade was not alone; he belonged to a network."

~~~

The Spas in Jakarta

Buddy, a Chinese-Indonesian who was my local contact in Jakarta, told me that most Chinese female sex workers in Indonesia were either in spas or a KTVs. After lunch, Buddy and I went to a spa located inside a hotel. We paid the entrance fee—about $5.50 per person—on the first floor and walked up to the lounge on the second floor. When we got there, we did not go to the locker room to put on robes as most customers usually do. We just walked straight into the lounge, found a table, and sat down. In the spacious lounge, there were more than twenty tables and a bar, and several groups of women were walking around or sitting on a couch.

Once we sat down, a young woman in a colorful and fashionable dress came over and greeted us. She said she was from Fuqing, Fujian, and she was a mommy here.[1] She asked us whether we would like to have women to accompany us, and we asked her to give us some time to think about it. She told us there are women from China, Indonesia, Thailand, Uzbekistan, and Spain. All the foreign women charge one and a half million rupiah (about $162) per session, and the local women cost $40, $85, or $108 per session. After she talked to us for another five minutes, she said she needed to take care of other clients and left, probably sensing that Buddy and I were not serious about asking for companionship.

Buddy and I ordered some drinks, and then just sat there and chatted while observing what was happening around us. Soon, three Chinese men in robes walked in, and the mommy from Fuqing rushed over to the men's table with a smile. After she talked to them for a few minutes, she waved to a group of Chinese women sitting on a large couch nearby, gesturing for them to stand up for the Chinese men to take a look at. Then the mommy asked all the Chinese women to come over to the men's table.

The three Chinese men sat there, sipping their drinks, smoking their cigarettes, and evaluating the women before them. The Fuqing mommy was busy introducing each and every woman to the men. The men spent more than ten minutes making a decision. Finally, they selected two women. The mommy worked very hard to find a woman for the third man, but he was just shaking his head constantly and finally gave up looking. The mommy asked the two selected women to sit down with the men, and ordered the rest to go back to their couch. The men and their hostesses laughed and chatted, while the third man sat there looking dejected. After a few minutes, the mommy led the couples to the back rooms. By then, it was around four in the afternoon, with not many visitors around. The chance of an interview seemed very unlikely, so Buddy and I walked over to the movie room inside the spa. It was a big and well-equipped movie room, but almost empty. We sat there and watched *Blood Diamond*. Soon, the third Chinese man wandered in and sat down, and after a while, fell asleep.

Meeting Cola in a Spa

The next day, Buddy drove me to another spa in his red Jeep. This spa was smaller than the one we had visited the day before, with only Chinese and Indonesian women. After we paid the entrance fee and went in, Buddy began to talk to a mommy in Indonesian; when she heard that I would pay for chatting, she nodded.

I picked one of the women among the more than dozen Chinese workers available. At that time, there were also more than twenty Indonesian women in the waiting area. The Chinese woman was in a black bikini, with a filmy silk wrap around her waist. She had long hair, and was wearing glitter on her eyes and face. After we sat at a table in a corner, I ordered two drinks.

I told the woman my story and asked her for her consent to participate in my study. She agreed to be interviewed. I asked her what her name was.

My name is Cola and I was born in a remote area near Huaihua, Hunan. My parents are both farmers. I have an older brother, and I am the daughter that my parents do not want. My dad is not good to me; he thinks daughters are like dirty water you throw away (after they are married); why should people waste money to educate their daughters? Plus, daughters are unlike sons; daughters can't continue the heritage. That's why I left home when I was very young. I was born in 1986, so I am twenty-one now. I completed vocational school; this means I studied for two years in a vocational school after middle school.

Raped at Fourteen

Cola lit a cigarette.

When I was fourteen, I and a female friend were both raped by two guys. After that, another guy brought me to Changde to engage in sex work, but I ran away and went back to Huaihua. Later, I traveled to a place near Guangzhou to work, and there I met a man who later brought me to Shenzhen to work in a sauna. When I resisted, he hit me. After I began to work in a sauna, he took away all my earnings. I was scared because he often threatened me: "If you run away, I will find you, and then I will hurt you real bad." I asked some of my clients to help me, but nobody was willing to help me. No women would like to be in this line of work!

I asked Cola about the man who forced her to engage in sex work.

The man who brought me into the sex trade was not alone; he belonged to a network. Members of the network went around looking for young women, and then tricked or forced these women to work in a variety of entertainment centers. They especially like to approach females who are working in the factories in Shenzhen and Dongguan. That's why they are most active near the industrial areas of those cities.

In China, there are many networks of men who travel to the remote areas or wander around the factories along the coastal areas looking for young women, then pretend to fall in love with the women, and pressure the women to engage in sex work to make money for them. Cola, unfortunately, ran into one of these men.

After working for a period of time, I escaped; I took a bus from the Louhu Station back to Huaihua. There, I ran into the man who brought me to Changde, and he again brought me to Guangzhou to sell sex. He began to worry about the man in Shenzhen, afraid that he might come looking for me, so he left me. After that, my only choice was to look for work in a sauna on my own.

From Shenzhen to Indonesia

Cola lit another cigarette.

Then I met a woman just back from Indonesia, and she hooked me up with a company there. That company became my agent. The company was recruiting a large number of women from China. I did not meet the Indonesian agent when I was still in China; we simply talked over the phone. The agent told me his company would refer us to the sex venues that they have contracts with.

The front door opened and several Indonesians walked in. After they sat down on a sofa, they began to select the women they wanted to take into rooms. The men probably had instructed the mommies that they only wanted Chinese women, because only the Chinese women went over to them. Cola continued to talk, completely ignoring the men who just walked in.

I flew to Jakarta in May 2007. My agent picked me up at the airport. I am not sure what my visa was good for. I think for two months and then maybe for two more months. After I got here, my agent asked me whether I would like to work in a nightclub or a KTV. I told him I preferred to work in a spa, and the agent also told me if I do not like to drink or use drugs, I have no choice but to work in a spa. My agent brought me to this spa, and after I checked into a dorm upstairs, I began working. They did not teach me anything here. I still do not know how to massage.

Sex For One and a Half Million Rupiah

There are primarily two ways for a Chinese woman to engage in sex work; one way is to work as a hostess in a nightclub or a KTV, mainly to sing, drink, and chat with clients, and occasionally go out with clients to engage in paid sex. Working in these venues requires hostesses to use drugs with clients sometimes, and also not to be upset when clients kiss and fondle them in the private rooms. The other way is to work in a massage parlor, a sauna, a spa, or an escort agency. The main activity in these venues is to engage in sexual intercourse. The two parties enter a room, remove their clothes, and have sex. Some women prefer nightclubs or KTVs because they think these venues are of higher quality, and they are less likely to harm themselves because they do not have to have sex with men so often. Some women like sauna or escort work better because they think there are fewer headaches in these types of venues, and there is no need for them to keep an intimate relationship with their clients. Cola (as well as Angie) belongs to the second type of women.

> When clients come here, they pick their masseuses in the waiting area. The entrance fee is $9, and the fee allows a client to use all the facilities here. If a client wants to have a masseuse, he needs to pay one and a half million rupiah [about $162], but no need to pay the entrance fee. Once a client and a masseuse enter a room, they have sex. I do not know massage, or know how to provide a variety of sex services. When I enter a room with a client, I just have sex with him.
>
> Of the $162 the client pays, I receive $81, and that's half of the money. A client may also give me tips, ranging from $30 to $200. Of course, this way of distributing the money is not fair. Half of the money is taken away by the spa, the mommy, and the agent. However, what can we do about this? We even need to pay for our food. The dorm upstairs is free, though. We get five days off every month, mainly to take a rest when we have our periods. If we are not going to work, we cannot go out on our own; we must be accompanied by our agents.
>
> I go to work around two in the afternoon every day, and work until eleven in the evening. Working here is like serving time in a prison; every day, it is upstairs or downstairs. So far, I've gone out only twice.

Tight Restrictions

When Cola talked about her lack of freedom of movement, she got very upset, and she picked up another cigarette. She said she was especially displeased with the spa management that day. She told me she was supposed to show up for work at 2:00 p.m. but was two minutes late and the spa fined her 500,000 rupiah ($54). Cola went wild and demanded the spa to send her back to China right away. Only after her mommy talked to her did she calm down.

> I see about one or two clients every day; three will be the most. Some days, I do not even have one client. I am considered to be one with

good business, and this means I at least see one client a day. Most of the customers are Chinese-Indonesians. Customers are in general not bad. They do not force us to do anything. Anyway, this is a legitimate spa. We have security people here and customers would not behave unreasonably here.

The mommy showed up, and she asked with a smile: "How are things going? You want to go inside?" I smiled back, saying: "No, not yet; we are having a good conversation now." The mommy did not give me a hard time; she just walked away.

We are not free here; even when we go out, we are always accompanied by someone. After work, we are also not allowed to go out; we have to stay in our dorm. The spa does not want us to have any interactions with clients outside the spa, otherwise they are not going to make money, and that is why they watch us closely. Besides, the spa took away our passports and visas; we only have copies of these documents.

Business people are always wary of not getting what they are supposed to get, and that is why the spa management does not want their masseuses to have any connections to their clients in private. However, if a business establishment takes away the women's passports and visas, this means there is a restriction on the women's freedom of movement, and according to the laws of many countries, this is considered human trafficking, even if the women are there voluntarily and have been informed of the nature of their work before they go overseas.

I send all my money to my mom. I plan to buy her a house and give her a lot of money so that she can live a good life. My mom is very good to me, and in my heart, her happiness is the most important thing. I always remember her pained expression when my dad asked her for money and she could not come up with any.

When Cola mentioned her mother, she was concerned, but when she talked about her father, she seemed like she did not care. I asked about her plans for the future.

I will try to go to another country. I do not want to come back to Indonesia again. I also want to live a normal life, find a man to marry me, and have my own family. I won't encourage anyone to enter this line of work. This is hard work, and I want to leave this occupation soon so that I can go learn some skills. Now, all I am thinking is to save $24,000 so that I can buy my mom a house. My older brother is still single, and my parents also expect me to buy my brother a house so that he can marry.

After the interview, I gave Cola $54, and she thanked me for the tip. She also said she would be going back to China soon.

A KTV with Rooms for Sex

LILY IN INDONESIA

Date: July 12, 2007
Place: A restaurant near a KTV in Jakarta
Name: Lily
Age: 31
Marital Status: Single

Born in Guangan, Sichuan. Dropped out of middle school; worked as a factory girl, hair salon assistant, and waitress. Became wayward after meeting her boyfriend. After being mistaken for a sex worker by police, entered prostitution. Worked in the sex industry in Singapore and Malaysia before Indonesia. This is her first trip to Indonesia, had been there for more than a month at time of interview.

"I am thirty-one now, you can't say I am young. How much longer can I do this?"

◠◡

KTVs in Jakarta

One hostess at a KTV first turned me down when I asked for an interview, but a day or two later she had changed her mind. Her name was Lily, and she met with me around three in the afternoon at a restaurant. She was wearing a T-shirt and blue jeans. The restaurant was on the street level of the building where her KTV was located, and since she was concerned about her colleagues seeing us together talking, we moved to the rear of the restaurant. Lily began.

> I was born in Guangan, Sichuan; it's about two hours by bus from Chongqing to Guangan. I am thirty-one now, single, and I quit school when I was in my first year in middle school.
> My parents are farmers, and they definitely like to have sons rather than daughters. I have a younger sister and a younger brother. My dad and mom did not want me and my sister when we were born, and that's why they continued to have children. When my little brother was born, they stopped having more children.

I had heard that story many times. As we were talking, Lily seemed to be keeping an eye on the entrance.

> After I quit school, I stayed home and did house chores. When I reached the age of sixteen, I went to Dongguan to work in a factory, and later moved to another city and worked in another factory. Working in a factory was hard, and I made only about $50 a month. Then I worked in a restaurant for $62 a month, but got into an argument with the brother of the boss. I left the restaurant.
> After that, I went to work for a hair salon for a few weeks. It was an illegal business [engaging in commercial sex besides the normal hair salon services], but I was only washing hair. Later, I went to work for a hotel as a waitress, and I met a guy who was a hustler. After I began to hang out with him, I stopped working.

Mistaken for a Sex Worker

Lily's experience was relatively typical for some women from rural areas of China: came out to work at a young age with little education or skills, found work in the factories in the coastal areas, entered the service industry, and so on. After they meet their boyfriends, they begin to change.

Once, I went shopping and was arrested by the police because they thought I was a prostitute. A friend of mine bailed me out for $180. The money was borrowed from someone. After that incident, a friend suggested I might as well work in a sauna, and I did.

I was trained for a month. For two years, I only did pure massage and was making up to $2,500 a month. I only did pure massage because I had a boyfriend at that time. After I split from my boyfriend, I began to provide special [sex] services and made good money. At that time, I was also crazy about gambling, so I pretty much gambled all my money away.

Not Easy to Make Money in China Anymore

Lily stressed that it was not easy to make money as a sex worker in China anymore. When China began to engage in economic reform, the sex business also began to develop. Eventually, sex ring operators were able to command high prices for sex services. Nowadays, there are many sex workers in China, so the price for sex services has declined. When I asked Lily whether she had been to other countries, she said she had been in Singapore and Malaysia before.

Before Indonesia, I was in Singapore, and I stayed there for twenty-eight days. I worked in a KTV located on Lorong 21. Besides sitting table, I also went out with clients because we could not do it inside. I spent $760 for my trip to Singapore, and that included the money for the air ticket. When I left Singapore, I netted about $2,000 after deducting the $760 expenses. Later, I went to Borneo, and when I was transiting in Malaysia, I worked as a hostess in Kota Kinabalu for a month. Business was very slow there; not only did I not make any money that trip, I even lost almost $400 after all the expenses were deducted from my earnings.

All the women who had worked in Singapore told me they made money there, but some of the women who went to Malaysia said they did not make much money. Lily is one of them. Kota Kinabalu is a major tourist attraction in Malaysia, but most Chinese women who had been there said the sex business involving them there was slow.

When I was in China, I met a woman who came back from Indonesia. She said she was willing to be my agent and brought me to Indonesia. She told me that I could make more than $2,500 a month there. That's how I got here in June 2007, and I have been here for more than a month now. She got me a tourist visa that allows me to stay here for six months. I do not know whether she personally applied for travel documents for me or there was someone else who did that. Initially, I was thinking about going back to Singapore, but I was having trouble getting the travel documents, and that's why I went to Malaysia instead, and then here. My agent charged me $1,250 for this trip, and I paid her when I was in China.

After a failed attempt to go to Singapore for the second time and losing money on a trip to Malaysia, Lily had no choice but to find another place to go, and she eventually ended up in Indonesia.

I arrived here with that returned sex worker who was my agent, and a forty-year-old female friend. We flew direct to Jakarta from Hong Kong. The agent initially referred the two of us to a nightclub, and they hired me but rejected my friend because they thought she was too old. So we went to a spa looking for a job and the same thing happened again; they wanted me but not my friend. Finally, someone introduced us to the KTV where I am working now, and luckily they hired both of us.

Sex inside the KTV

Lily could have worked in a nightclub or a spa, but she decided to work in a KTV so that she could be with a friend. I asked Lily what it was like to work in a KTV.

Every day I get up around three in the afternoon, eat something, and then prepare to go to work. I start work around seven to eight in the evening, and go back to my dorm in the early morning. The dorm is right above the KTV, and it is comfortable; at least both the room and the food are free.

Here, I can make about $1,500 a month. I send home about $250 every month. It's hard to say how many clients I have a day; when business is really slow, I do not have one client for a few days. The clients are alright; they are not as good as those in Singapore, but much better than those in China and Malaysia.

The KTV where Lily worked had back rooms for clients to have sex with the hostesses. A mommy of the KTV had told me about this when I talked to her a couple of days ago. She is a Chinese-Indonesian and she told me in broken Chinese, "If a client wants to do it [have sex], we got rooms inside the KTV to do it, no need to go outside. The price is $160, plus $6 for the room." No wonder the Indonesian police had been very active in raiding these KTVs recently; they must have suspected that hostesses were selling sex inside these premises. As a result, business for the KTVs had been in significant decline. I asked Lily whether she felt like she was free to move around. Many Chinese women in Indonesia told me they were not.

We are not that free in Indonesia. First, we live in the dorm provided to us by our KTV employer, and the dorm is located above the KTV, so we do not go out that often. Second, our passports and visas are being taken care of by our company.

Lily shook her head, and it was clear that she felt powerless with the situation she was in. I asked Lily about her future.

It's hard to say what my plan is for the future because I am here for only a month. If it is good working here, I will come back. If not, I won't. I still want to marry; I am thirty-one now, you can't say I am young. How much longer can I do this? Because I like to gamble and had a boyfriend to support, I haven't been able to save money or buy an apartment in Shenzhen.

Lily appeared depressed talking about this. She had been engaged in sex work for more than ten years, and yet she was still pretty much empty-handed. She wanted to marry, yet there was no one to marry.

Thinking the Most Romantic Thing

NA NA IN LOS ANGELES

Date: March 3, 2008
Place: An apartment in Rosemead, Los Angeles
Name: Na Na
Age: 28
Marital Status: Single

Born in Dalian, Liaoning. Graduated from college with a BA in international business law. Lived with boyfriend, split after he fell in love with some one else. Had an abortion. Spent about $40,000 to be smuggled into the United States. Currently selling sex in a rented apartment in Los Angeles.

"To my surprise, all men are alike, regardless of their age."

〜

Chinese on the West Coast of the United States

In the United States, the largest numbers of Chinese live in Los Angeles and New York. On the West Coast, there are also many Chinese in San Francisco, San Diego, San Jose, and Oakland. My sister and her family have lived in Los Angeles for many years, so I was relatively familiar with the city.

I flew from New York to Los Angeles, rented a car at the airport, and drove it to a hotel in San Gabriel. There are many Chinese in San Gabriel, who along with those in Monterey Park, Alhambra, and Rosemead constitute a major Chinese community in the County of Los Angeles. In these four cities, not only are there many immigrants from China, Taiwan, and Hong Kong but also a substantial number of Vietnamese and Vietnamese-Chinese. Most Chinese immigrants from China in Los Angeles are from northeastern China. In New York, however, most are from Fujian and Guangdong (southeastern China).

After I told her the purpose of my trip to Los Angeles, my sister told me to stay in a reputable hotel in San Gabriel. Many Chinese businesses are located nearby, and also a large number of Chinese-owned sex venues. I checked in, then went to a nearby bookstore and bought some Chinese newspapers: the *World Journal*, the *Sing Tao Daily*, the *International Daily News*, and the *Liberty Times*. I found many classified ads related to commercial sex in the first two newspapers; one can find not only Chinese women from those ads but also women from Taiwan, South Korea, Japan, and Malaysia. I was reassured; finding Chinese sex workers in the Los Angeles area would not be a problem. I ate dinner in a nearby restaurant and went to bed early.

Young and Beautiful, Skin White as Snow

The next day after lunch, I began to read the sex ads carefully. I made seven or eight calls, but none of them brought any results (some calls were not answered, some reached only answering machines, my cell phone area code may have raised suspicions, etc.). Then I saw the following ad and made another call.

> Young and Beautiful
> Skin White as Snow
> xxx-xxx-xxxx
> Outcall also

A woman answered the phone. After a brief conversation, I asked her the price, and she said $120. The kind of money she charged assured me that she was engaged in commercial sex. When I asked her where she was located, she ignored my question and instead asked me where I was calling from. When I told her the name of my hotel in San Gabriel, she said it was very easy for me to get to her place and that it would take only a few minutes to get there. She asked me whether I was driving. When I said yes, she asked me to go east from the hotel, make a couple of turns, and call her again.

I stopped the car and called after following her directions. She asked me to keep going, and after a traffic light and two stop signs, call her again. When I called the third time, she gave me even more instructions and finally told me to wait for her in front of apartment building number 248. I parked the car, got out, and waited. After a few minutes, a woman showed up from behind and greeted me, and then led me to her apartment deep inside a complex. It was around two in the afternoon, and I did not see anyone else around.

Na Na from Dalian

She was tall and slim, wearing jeans and a tight white T-shirt with a conspicuous black bra underneath. Her hair was neatly tied into a pony tail. The sun was shining, and in the bright daylight her skin looked pale and dry.

She took me to a two-story apartment and asked whether I would like to shower first. When I said no, she led me into her bedroom after asking me to remove my shoes. Her bedroom was on the first floor, small and neat, with a bathroom. The blinds were pulled down.

Once we were inside the room, I explained to her who I was, the research project I was working on, and so on. She agreed to participate in my study, calmly nodding her head without much hesitation. However, she asked me to pay her first, insisting that it was her rule: first time visitors must pay first. I paid her $120 and just hoped that she would still be cooperative after taking my money.

My name is Na Na, born in Dalian. I am twenty-eight, single. My parents are retired; they retired when they were in their forties. They were both midlevel government employees. I am their only child.

I graduated from college with a degree in international business law. After graduation, I worked for a real estate company owned by a friend of my boyfriend. I met my boyfriend when we were in college. Later, we lived together. He was a general manager of a company, making lots of money.

Na Na seemed to be quite proud when she mentioned her boyfriend. I wondered how a woman with such a good start in life ended up selling sex in a faraway country.

We were deeply in love then and I became pregnant with his child, but I had an abortion.

When Na Na said that, it was clear that she did not think it was a big deal.

Not long after we started living together, my boyfriend often did not come home after he went to business dinner parties. He called and said he had too much to drink, so he found a sauna to take a shower, a massage, and some sleep and he won't be coming home. In fact, at that time, he met an eighteen-year-old singer, rented an apartment for her, and he was spending nights at her place.

A Bloody Confrontation

At that point, Na Na became very emotional. When she referred to the singer who stole her man, her face turned red.

That young woman got pregnant, so the three of us had a meeting to sort things out. That woman got hysterical; she picked up a bottle, smashed it, and then cut her wrist with the broken glass. Then she asked me whether I would also die for my boyfriend. I did not back off; I also slashed my wrist with a piece of glass.

Na Na was talking very fast, using her hands to show me how two females were engaged in a showdown for a male, when her cell phone rang. Someone was calling to ask for directions to her place, but once the caller heard that it would cost $120 per session, he backed off.

Later, my boyfriend calmed that woman down and persuaded her to have an abortion. However, after that incident, he was still reluctant to leave her. I was thinking, if he was fooling around with other women before our marriage, how can I be sure he will be loyal to me after the marriage. So I left him. I quit my job and went home.

My boyfriend was still young—about thirty—so I had thought he wouldn't be like those men in their forties running around, womanizing. To my surprise, all men are alike, regardless of their age. My boyfriend was also well educated, and he had such a good job. I never would have imagined our relationship would end like this. That experience was a major blow to me.

Getting Abroad

Na Na sighed.

After I split with my boyfriend, I became very active in finding a way to go overseas, never mind that everyone in China wants to go abroad. I thought about this before, but because my TOEFL and GRE scores were low, I knew I wouldn't receive any scholarships.[1]

After I graduated from college, I did take the exam for a law license. When I took it the first time, I only needed four more points to pass it. When I tried the second and third time, my scores got worse and worse. In China, I do not have a future without a license to practice law.

Na Na was candid about the predicament she was in; no wonder she had been working for a real estate company after graduating from college with a law degree.

When a friend came back from the United States, I asked her how she got there. She said a company helped her, and soon introduced me to people from that company. They said I was too young to go to the

United States. They could only help people who were thirty-five or older. At that time, I was only twenty-five or twenty-six. They said if I really wanted to go, they still could help me but it would cost more. They charged most people $25,000, but I had to pay an extra $12,500 because they had to change all the information in my household registration and come up with a set of personal information. All the new documents would show that I was over thirty. That's how I was able to come to the United States. The company is also located in Dalian.

These so-called companies or brokers in China are really incredible; as long as the price is right, they can help anyone go to any country. Na Na must have been determined to leave China if she was willing to pay $12,500 more for the trip.

I waited for almost a year, because the broker needed a lot of time to make all the arrangements. I arrived here with a tourist visa in April 2007; after being here for six months, I extended my visa for another six months. So far, my visa is still valid. Right now, I want to find someone to marry for real so that I can apply for a green card [permanent resident status].

New York: Not as Good as Dalian

Na Na was pretty good at expressing herself, and when she talked, she was right to the point. I thought she should able to finish her story within the time limit.

I came here alone. I flew to New York from China, and I stayed in Flushing [New York] for a week. There, I saw many minorities, and it was a dirty and chaotic place. It was not as good as our Dalian. I was scared every time I stepped out of my house, and I was worried I would be robbed when I took the subway. A friend suggested that I go to Los Angeles and said she could introduce me to a friend there.

Many newly arrived immigrants from China are shocked when they first set foot in Flushing, wondering how there is such a community in a developed country like the United States.

When I arrived in Los Angeles, I found a job as a waitress. It was hard work; when I got home every night, my feet hurt because of all the walking in the restaurant.

From Restaurant to Nightclub

Later, I met a manager from a nightclub. He invited me to work in his nightclub as a hostess, and assured me it would be easy work and a lot more money. That's why after three months in America, I started to work in a nightclub.

I worked for a month in that nightclub, and I was drunk like crazy every night. A doctor told me I should not drink like that anymore. Besides, I really can't stay up late every night. That's why I decided to do pure massage. After working as a masseuse for a while, I occasionally went out with my customers to a nearby hotel to have sex.

Na Na's cell phone rang again. She told the caller she was busy and asked him to call back in half an hour.

When I was working in the nightclub, I went out with a customer once in a while. Initially, I was reluctant to go out, but my mommy said, "You had a boyfriend before, right? What's the difference between that and going out with a customer? Why can't you go out? That guy who wants to go out with you is a rich man, why don't you go?" I had no choice but to go out. When I went out for the first time, we did not do anything—just eat and chat.

When Na Na imitated how her mommy tried to coerce her to go out with a customer, she talked very fast in a high-pitched voice, and she put one hand on her waist and waved the other in front of my face. Her performance made me laugh.

Only Chinese Clients

I asked Na Na how she was running her current business.

A friend rents this place for $1,600 a month, and I pay half of the rent. I put an ad in the newspapers, and when a client walks in, I ask him whether he wants to take a bath first. After that, I will give him a little massage, and then do it. I only do regular sex.

Every day, I come here around two in the afternoon. I live somewhere else. I do not have a car; so I rely on a limousine service to move back and forth between this place and my home.

It's hard to say how many men I see each day. Usually, I have one or two clients a day. When business is good, I might have three or four clients a day. I am very cautious. If I think the caller is difficult, I would rather not do business with him. Besides, I only advertise my services in the Chinese newspapers and do business only with Chinese clients. The clients are from China, Taiwan, and Hong Kong.

While Na Na was seeing clients downstairs, her friend was doing the same upstairs. They all have their own bedroom and bathroom, so there was no conflict between them. It was not clear why Na Na had to rent another place; it could be for safety and comfort. I asked how much she is making now.

I charge $120 per session, and I keep all of it. I only have to share the rent with my friend. I make about six to seven thousand a month. When I was with the nightclub, I earned only $20 per table as hostess, but I was able to take home one to two hundred daily. When I was doing pure massage, I also made about one to two hundred every day.

I spent $40,000 to come to America. I borrowed all the money and I had to pay interest. You can say I am a big spender. I like shopping, and also eating Japanese food. I did send money home to repay the debt, and so far, I have cleared half of it. I do not dare send all the money I make here home, worrying that my family will be suspicious and wondering what the hell I am doing here to make this kind of money.

Young and Pretty Women Are All Doing This

Na Na said she would rather take it slow repaying the debt (and pay more interest as a result) than alarm her family by making unusually large payments. I asked Na Na whether she knew any Chinese women in Los Angeles who were trafficked. She looked shocked.

It is not possible to deceive or force someone to enter this line of work here. If a woman says she is being deceived or forced, it must be a lie. She must have been coached by other women about what to tell the police if she is arrested. Other women have told me this. I can assure you that there are no trafficked victims in Los Angeles, just many willing sex workers here. In any case, most of the young pretty Chinese women you see here in Los Angeles are involved in this occupation.

Na Na seemed like she knew what she was saying. However, I am not sure it is true that so many Chinese women in Los Angeles are in the sex business. I asked Na Na about her plans for the future.

I want to marry someone and get a green card. I still dream about having true love. Whenever I see old, loving couples, I can't help but envy what they have. I also hope that when I am old, and my hair turns gray, and I can't walk anymore, there will be a man who treats me like I am his most precious thing, and we will be sharing all the good memories. Finding someone to marry is now the most urgent thing for me to do.

As Na Na was talking, her eyes were looking up as if she was dreaming about the kind of endless love depicted in a popular Chinese song, "The Most Romantic Thing."

I realized that I was almost running out of time, so I asked Na Na whether she regretted coming to the US.

I regret coming here. When I was in China, I did not know I would end up like this in America. Here, I am very lonely because I have no friends or relatives. I hope I can leave this line of work soon.

When Na Na talked about how lonely she was here, she lowered her head and sighed deeply.

CHAPTER 16

Making $20,000 a Month

KELLY IN LOS ANGELES

Date: March 8, 2008
Place: A house in San Gabriel, Los Angeles
Name: Kelly
Age: 36
Marital Status: Married, with a ten-year-old daughter

Born in Beijing, graduated from occupational school specializing in preliminary education. Was a preschool teacher for ten years. Came to the United States after catching husband sleeping with other women. In Los Angeles, worked in a restaurant and then a massage parlor. Currently running her own house.

"Business was very good when I began to rotate among houses; I had more than ten clients a day, so I made a lot of money then."

Chinese "Houses" in Los Angeles

In Los Angeles, Chinese people in the sex industry like to use the word "house" for the place where sexual transactions are conducted.

While I was still in the city, I called more phone numbers. Around three o'clock one afternoon, I found the following ad in the *World Journal*, the Taiwan-based newspaper with the largest circulation in North America.

White Snow, Newly Opened
Beautiful Woman in a Quiet Environment
Excellent Service
xxx-xxx-xxxx

A woman answered my call, and after a short conversation said her price was $100. She told me her address, only a few blocks from my hotel. Her place was located in a large residential area packed with many one-family houses and townhouses. I parked my car and followed a narrow walkway which led me to rows of townhouses.

I found the address and rang the bell, and a woman quickly opened the door. Once I got inside, she asked me to take off my shoes, and then took me upstairs. I had a quick look at the first floor: living room, bedroom, and bathroom. Once we entered a bedroom on the second floor, she asked me whether I wanted to take a shower. I said no and told her about my research project. Once she heard the word "interview," she got nervous, but after some hesitation, she gave me her consent to be interviewed.

Her bedroom was very clean and decorated like a typical bedroom. She was wearing a low-neck T-shirt and three-quarter pants. After she sat down on the bed and I sat in a chair, I asked her where she was from.

My name is Kelly; I was born in Beijing. I am thirty-six, married, and my husband and our ten-year-old daughter are in China. My parents were government employees. I also had a younger brother. Our family was neither rich nor poor; we were okay.

It was around four in the afternoon and very quiet inside the house. Kelly seemed a little nervous about talking to me; she probably had never encountered this kind of request in the past. However, she was poised and constantly observing me, trying to figure out what kind of person I really was.

I graduated from a vocational school, majoring in elementary education. I worked in a preschool for almost ten years after I graduated. I made about $300 a month.

Hopeless in China

A woman who worked as a preschool teacher for ten years in China was now selling sex in the United States. "What a change," I thought to myself.

I married when I was twenty-four. My husband was a taxi driver. The two of us were not making enough money. I got into an argument with the management in my work unit and I quit. At that point, my husband was beginning to patronize sex venues in our area. I was disappointed with him, so I suggested that one of us must go out to make money. He was a conservative person with no guts, so of course I was the one who had to go out. The bottom line was, I decided that I would give it a try. In China, government officials are so corrupt, there is no hope for ordinary people. But I just happened to know a broker who said he could help me come to America, so I came.

Kelly had appeared to be at ease before this. When she talked about corruption in China, she seemed frustrated and very upset. The same was true when she talked about her husband.

This company first helped me go to Europe and Japan as a tourist. After I had those travel records, there was a better chance that I would be able to get a US visa. If you are Chinese and have never been overseas, the US officials think that once you are here, you will never go back.

These brokers in China are smart. Because all the expenses are paid by their clients—Chinese citizens desperate to find a way to go to the United States—the brokers try to come up with a flawless plan, even if this means the person applying for a US visa has to spend more money.

I arrived here in February 2006 with a business visa, valid for three months. It took about a year to obtain the visa. I had an interview at the US embassy in Beijing, accompanied by two men: one was the director of a factory and the other, the deputy director of that factory. I was their secretary. In fact, it was all fake. We said we were going to Las Vegas for a trade fair.

In the early 1990s, a large number of Fujianese were smuggled into the United States by boat or via the land route across the Mexico-US border. Chinese citizens from the northeast, Beijing, and Shanghai were more likely to fly into the United States as members of a business delegation or as students.

We flew from Beijing to Shanghai to Los Angeles, and then we did show up briefly at the exhibition in Las Vegas. A man in Los Angeles who was working for the broker company in China helped in the process.

A Family Hotel

When Chinese citizens arrive in the United States for the first time, it is crucial to have someone help them get around. Kelly's broker in China was thoughtful enough to have someone in Los Angeles greet her and her partners at the airport.

After the trade fair in Las Vegas, I returned to Los Angeles and checked into a family hotel, also arranged by the Los Angeles broker. It cost $10 a day. When I was there, a man who was also staying there was very nice to me and said I should learn to drive and get my license before my business visa expired. He said the driver's license will be very useful for me in the future. After taking the driving lessons, I got my license after taking the road test four times.[1]

Kelly became more relaxed, and we were like two friends having a nice conversation. I was familiar with these so-called family hotels in New York, so I understood what Kelly was talking about. A family hotel is just a room that some landlords rent out to new immigrants on a temporary basis. Landlords may even convert their own living rooms and garages into living quarters for temporary tenants. I visited a family hotel in Los Angeles. The Chinese landlord and his family—all six of them—lived on the second floor of a townhouse, while the living room, kitchen, and garage on the first floor were used to accommodate six male and female immigrants, all from China.

> After checking into that family hotel, at first I worked as a waitress in a restaurant. I worked for seven days and quit because one, it was hard work, and two, the men in the kitchen were sexually harassing me all the time. I can't work under such circumstances!

From Restaurant to House

> After I quit the job at the restaurant, I called a massage parlor. When I got there, the owner told me if I do only massage, I am not going to make much money and then she talked me into doing more. After I worked there for a few days, I began to do full set.

Kelly's experience is rather typical for many new, female immigrants. Most of them would like to engage in normal, legitimate work after they arrive, but then discover they have to engage in some type of semi-legitimate work to survive, then further discover if they are willing to engage in sex work they can make much, much more. When Kelly was talking about her experience moving from restaurant work to sex work, it sounded like an inevitable chain of events.

> I did full set in a house, and there was only me and my female boss. At that point you can say I was an in-house woman, meaning I saw clients in one particular house, and I went back to my place to sleep after work.
>   At that house, the clients paid $100 per session; I got $70 and the boss took $30. Some of the clients gave me tips, about $10 or $20. I did not see many clients in that house; I had about three every day.

CHAPTER 16

Rotating among Houses

After working in that house for three months, some limousine drivers suggested I should rotate among houses, meaning I should see clients in several houses in the same day. Normally, a big house has a few bedrooms, but they may only have one on-duty woman, and when there is more than one client, they will ask a woman from the outside for help. In a big house, a client pays $120; the house takes $40, and I get $80. I need to pay a limousine driver $5 to drive me to a house, and then another $5 to go to another house. At any rate, it cost me $10 in limousine fees per job.

Like Kelly, most Chinese women in Los Angeles work as on-duty sex workers first because they are new here, and they do not have driver's licenses and cars. However, after a short period of time, they become familiar with their environment and will rely on limousine drivers to take them to several houses, so that they can entertain more clients. Once they receive their licenses, they buy used cars and stop relying on the limousine services to travel from house to house. After they make enough money, they will buy brand new luxury vehicles.

Business was very good when I began to rotate among houses; I had more than ten clients a day, so I made a lot of money then. I got $80 per job, plus $20 tips, so I made $100 per job. I will make $1,000 if I do ten jobs, and after deducting the $100 I spend on limousine daily, I will take home $900 every day. At that time, making $20,000 a month was not a problem. Later, I bought a car and drove it to work, and it saved me $100 a day in limousine money. Running among houses all day and having to see so many clients of course took a toll on me, but as long as I was making money, that was fine.

Kelly got excited when she talked about how much money she once made, especially when she said she was making more than $20,000 a month. There are not many people in America making this kind of money. No wonder so many female immigrants in the United States are being lured into the sex trade by "masseuse" ads in the newspapers. In these ads, there will be phrases like "One thousand dollars a day," "$30,000 a month guaranteed," "No experience needed," "No immigration status check," and "Absolutely confidential." These ads naturally attract large numbers of young women who have labored in restaurants or garment factories for one to two thousand dollars a month. Some of them may call the numbers on these ads just out of curiosity, but once they make the call, they are surprised to find how quickly they are drawn into this profession.

I rotated among houses for several months. I later had a major medical operation, and because I did not have any medical insurance, I spent a large sum of money. I also did not work for a few months. I returned to work last year, and during that time, business was good and I made a lot of money.

I moved into this townhouse not long ago because this is bigger than where I used to live. However, once I moved in, there were rumors that I was using my townhouse to operate a sex business, so all the big houses stopped calling me. I was kind of being forced to open my own house. I see clients on my own, and if there are too many clients, I also ask for help outside, so you can say my place is also a house. My business is not that good; the first day I got seven customers, but after that, only about four a day.

Opening a House

I asked Kelly how much her rent was and how she conducted her sex business.

I rented this place for $1,600 a month. I use one bedroom for business and another for me to sleep at night. In this complex, there are many houses.

I operate my place like this. Once a client walks in, I ask him to pay me $100. And then I ask him to take a shower. After that, I massage him for about ten minutes, put a condom on him, and do some blowing before doing it. Altogether it takes about twenty minutes.

From Kelly's description, it sounded like seeing a client was a simple process and there were not many sexual services to speak of.[2]

All of a sudden, Kelly got up and said, "Since we are just talking, why don't we go to the living room?" I agreed. From her point of view, if I was not there to buy sex, why take the risk of being alone with me in a bedroom? What if the police showed up?

When we got to the living room, I sat down on a sofa and Kelly sat on the floor by the coffee table. She picked up some *World Journal* newspapers and taught me how to read (and understand) the sex ads listed there: the ads belonging to the big houses, the ads by individual sex workers, the ads placed by male house owners (those that are explicit), and by female house owners (those that are subtle).

I only advertise my service in the Chinese newspapers because I do not want to do business with foreigners [whites]—plus a foreigner could be a cop. I also never engaged in sex work outside of Los Angeles. I am afraid to do it somewhere else because I worry that bad things can happen if I do this in an unfamiliar place.

Every day, I get up early in the morning and then wait for calls. If I am free, I also cook and clean the house. Well, I think it is good for me to be here in America because I work harder; when I was in China, I did not do any house chores. Plus, I do not play mahjong here as often as in China. In the evenings, limousine drivers and sex workers may come to my place to drink and chat.

Now I have about four clients every day. When I was running from house to house in the past, I had more than ten a day, and some of them were foreigners. Now, all my clients are Chinese, mostly from Taiwan and Hong Kong.

Difficult Clients

My clients are nice, I have not run into a really bad one. I saw a client from China this morning, and he removed the condom while we were having sex. Luckily, I noticed that and I told him he can't do that. Even so, it really bothered me. I also have not run into really sick clients, only those who ask me to wear high-heeled shoes. Some men ask me to reduce the price when we are talking over the phone, and I do not want this kind of client. But if a person shows up and says he does not have enough money and asks me to charge a little less, like $80 or $90, I will say fine.

I had never been subjected to client violence. Having said this, when I was rotating among several houses, I met a man who was very drunk. He wouldn't ejaculate after a long time, so I told him I can't go on like this. He said, "I came here to fuck you—how can you say you cannot stand it anymore?" I told him he should not say something that hurts my dignity, and he said women like us had no dignity to speak of. And then he was about to hit me, so I rushed out of the room to avoid being assaulted.

Kelly was apparently very angry and felt humiliated when she recalled this incident. I turned my focus to money issues, such as how much she had to pay to come to America, how much she was making, and how was she managing her money.

Altogether it cost me more than $30,000 to come to America, including the expenses for the trips to Japan and Europe. I sold an old house inherited from my parents for a little less than $30,000 and used all that money to help me come here.

Now, after deducting all my expenses, I make about eight or nine thousand dollars a month. I save as much as I can and send the money back to China, so that I can buy a house in Beijing one day. I drink beer regularly, and I go to Las Vegas occasionally to gamble. However, I do not play mahjong as often as I did in China.

I asked Kelly whether she was ever arrested, mainly because US authorities were being very aggressive over the past few years in cracking down on Asian sex venues.

The one thing that concerns me the most is the police. Every day when I answer the phone, I am very nervous. That's why I have three cell phones. The first one is the number in the newspaper ad, and I am always very careful whenever I am talking on that phone. After a customer comes for the first time, and if I like him, I will give him my business card with the second cell phone number on it. I am always very comfortable talking to anyone on this phone. The third one is an old cell phone. I am still using it because I don't want to lose contact with my old customers. I have always been very careful, and I was lucky, so I was never arrested or robbed.

Occasionally, I will see clients in their hotel rooms, and I charge $150 for that. Normally, I will try my best not to go to a hotel—I am afraid it is a police sting operation. In general, if the man asking me to come to his hotel room is from China, I will go; if he is from either Hong Kong or Taiwan, I don't. The reason is because many Chinese cops in Los Angeles speak Cantonese, but they will tell us they are tourists from Hong Kong.

"Kelly; Free Ride"

Kelly got up, walked over to the kitchen, picked up a business card, and handed it to me. On the card, only a phone number and the words "Kelly; Free Ride" were printed. She said: "Some clients are restaurant workers or they are staying in a family hotel. They want to come here, but they do not have cars. I will go pick them up, and drive them back later." I asked her whether there are women from China tricked or forced into prostitution in the United States, and she gave me the following firm answer.

How can anyone deceive a woman into coming to the United States? Don't forget, you need to go to the American embassy, fill out a lot of forms, go through many processes, and you must obtain a visa. How can someone be deceived into going through all these difficulties?

I do sex work because I want to make money! Women like us, what else can we do to make this kind of money? Anyhow, this is just a transition in life, a means to achieve a goal, and I am not going to do this forever. Here in Los Angeles, I think more than 90 percent of [Chinese] women are engaged in sex work. The women who are now owners of beauty parlors, restaurants, and big houses are all former sex workers; they change their careers after they make enough money.

Kelly looked like she knew what she was doing and how to get what she wants. She also felt that selling sex is no big deal and that many women are doing it in secret. I asked about her future plans.

My business visa will expire soon. Meanwhile, I found a church to help me apply for political asylum—I told them I was persecuted in China because I was a Christian.[3] I expect to receive my green card any time now. I am also applying for my daughter to join me. My husband probably won't be coming; he said he does not like America. But what could he do here anyway? Once my daughter is here, I will quit this work and do something else. As far as my husband is concerned, it doesn't matter whether he comes or not.

I do not regret coming to America, or entering this line of work. This is just temporary, anyway. This is a money-making job; it is also a hard job.

At the end of our interview, I gave $100 to Kelly. When I was about to leave, she gave me many suggestions on how to approach sex workers for an interview. I thanked her and left.

More than Massage in a Massage Parlor

ANITA IN NEW JERSEY

Date: October 20, 2007
Place: A massage parlor in northern New Jersey
Name: Anita
Age: 38
Marital Status: Married, with a fifteen-year-old son

Born in Tianjin. Graduated from middle school. Engaged in various kinds of work in China, but not sex work. Worked as a nanny upon arriving in the United States, turned to sex work not long after. Currently working in a massage parlor in northern New Jersey.

"I told myself I spent $25,400 to come to the United States, yet I was subjected to such humiliation; I felt so bad for myself."

∽

Massage Parlors in New Jersey

My university (Rutgers) is located in Newark, New Jersey, about a twenty-minute drive from New York City. New York City's Chinatown on the Lower East Side of Manhattan is the largest Chinese community in North America. As more and more Chinese immigrants arrived in the United States over the past three decades, a second Chinatown was established in Flushing, Queens, and a third in Sunset Park, Brooklyn.[1] There are also many Chinese living in the towns of northern New Jersey, an area that is very close to New York City.

Many Chinese-owned adult entertainment venues (such as spas, KTVs, nightclubs, and massage parlors) exist in the greater metropolitan area, though they tend to be concentrated in the three Chinatowns mentioned above. In New Jersey, the majority of Asian (mainly Chinese and Korean) sex venues are massage parlors.

As I had done in the West Coast, I looked at newspaper ads for places where I might locate subjects to interview. One day, after browsing through the sex ads in the World Journal, I decided to call a massage parlor located not far from my university. It was around four in the afternoon. A woman who spoke fluent Chinese answered the phone. I asked her for the address, but she only told me to go to a particular street number on a particular street and then she would meet me there. It was obvious she was not willing to tell me the exact location of her business.

It took me about twelve minutes to travel to the destination by car. After I parked my car, I called her again from the place where I was to meet her: a retail store facing a street. Soon, a middle-aged Chinese woman approached and asked me to follow her. We entered a nondescript building from a side entrance, and after passing through a few offices and an unmarked door, arrived at the massage parlor. It was clear that this was an almost ideal location for a sex venue: near a major street but off the street, tucked discreetly inside an office building where many small companies were located, and close to a parking lot.

Once inside, there was a visitor area, very plain, with a small table and an incense burner and a plate of fruit on top. There was a strong smell of incense. The woman poured a cup of water from a water cooler and promptly brought me into a room with a massage table, a chair, and a nightstand. A small radio, a dim lamp, a box of tissues, and a bottle of baby oil were on top of the nightstand. The radio was on, but the volume was kept relatively low.

Mary the Boss

The woman asked me whether I would like to take a shower, and when I said no, she asked to be paid $50 for fifty minutes, or one session, of massage. She said the two workers she had were both working and she could give me a massage while waiting. I politely declined her offer but asked to chat with her instead. She readily agreed; she could also answer the phone if someone called because she had a cordless phone with her. While we were talking, her phone was ringing all the time; she tried her best to answer callers' questions with her limited English.

The owner was in her late thirties, wore a black T-shirt, black jeans, and no makeup. She was friendly and respectful, and when she talked, she smiled a lot. She said her name was Mary and she had been living in the United States for twelve years. She worked in a restaurant after she got here but began to sell sex not long after that. She opened this massage parlor more than a year ago, and her major expense was advertising; it cost her several thousand dollars a month to advertise her business in English and Chinese newspapers and on the Internet.

Not long after, I heard a client about to leave, and Mary went out to say goodbye. After a few minutes, another woman appeared, younger and of mixed ethnicity. Her Chinese sounded strange to me, and I quickly learned she was from China, but was an ethnic Korean from the border area of Jilin Province. I was concerned that the interview will not be able to proceed smoothly if she could not express herself well in Chinese, so I went out to ask Mary whether I could wait for the other masseuse. I did not say why, but she said it would be fine.

Anita from Tianjin

Soon, another woman walked in; she spoke fluent Chinese and looked Chinese. I told her about my research project, asked her to participate in my study, and assured her she would be paid. She agreed and added something like, "Well, I can take this opportunity to get many things off my chest." After she sat on the massage table and I on a chair, I asked her to introduce herself.

My name is Anita, born in Tianjin. I am thirty-eight, married, with a fifteen-year-old son. Both my husband and my son are in China. My father was a car repairman for a government unit, and my mother a packaging employee for another government unit. We had four girls in our family; I am the youngest. When I was young, our family was not that bad off financially.

While Anita and I were talking, I heard more noises outside; it sounded like Mary was welcoming another visitor. He sounded like a Filipino. Then, the place became quiet again.

I was sixteen when I graduated from a middle school. After school, I worked for a government unit in Tianjin, making only $4 a month. But I worked there until I got married at the age of twenty-three. My husband was a street peddler. After I married, I quit my job. I gave birth two years later, and after another year, I came out to work again because my husband stopped working as a peddler. Besides, he never gave me any money to spend.

Working at a Health Center in Tianjin

Anita appeared to be older than thirty-eight. Many sex workers I have encountered in the United States told me they regularly understate their age.

I went to work for a health center in Tianjin. It was a large business operation; the center had a restaurant, a karaoke, and a massage place with special service. I worked as a waitress there; most of the sex workers were from northeastern China.

They charged $13 per session for massage, and a client must pay for two sessions per visit. For sex service, the extra charge was $60, so it cost a man about $86 if he wanted to have sex. That was 1996, so at that point in time, that establishment was considered very high class. Anyway, the owner was well-connected, so he did whatever he wanted. Nevertheless, it got into trouble [with the police] later, so I left.

Later, I found a job as a hostess in a music hall, and I drank, sang, and chatted with clients. After working there for a while, my husband and I had a big argument, and I quit.

Anita was very precise when she talked about her past. I began to get nervous because I knew I did not have unlimited time.

Then I became a taxi driver. We bought a taxi and my husband and I drove two different shifts. I worked very hard as a taxi driver, but my husband was a little lackluster. Business was quite good at the beginning, but after two years we sold our taxi—too much competition.

After that, I worked for a government unit again, this time at a food factory. I was making only $95 a month. Later, I became a saleslady and increased my monthly income to almost $240.

I wanted to come to the US since 2002, but I did not have the money to pay for the trip, so it was just a dream. Later, my sister loaned me money for the trip. A travel agency in Tianjin said they could help, but they required that I have records of going abroad twice. Therefore I went abroad twice in order to come here.

Entering the United States

The travel agency applied for a business visa for me to come to the US, but it was rejected by the US embassy; then the agency applied for a tourist visa for me and that was issued. There were more than twenty people on the tour going to the US.

Our group entered the United States in Hawaii. At the airport, American immigration officials asked me many questions and searched my luggage thoroughly. It was very frustrating; I decided that I wouldn't be going back to China no matter what. Originally, the plan was for us to go back to China, apply for a US business visa for the second time, go to the US for a second time, and stay there for good. This way, we can get back $3,600 from our travel agency. However, once we got here the first time and realized how many hurdles we have to go through to enter the US, and the fact that making $3,600 in the US was not going to be that difficult, we decided not to go back. There was a man from Tianjin in our group, and once he heard that I wasn't going back, he also decided the same. Another man left the group and disappeared once we arrived in Hawaii; I heard that he wanted to go to Canada.

Anita was talking about her trip to America in a very specific way, and it was hard for me to rush her, so I let her talk.

To come here, I spent altogether $25,400, including $2,400 for an initial trip to Europe, Singapore, and Malaysia. I paid the travel agency in Tianjin $23,000, and this money included $3,600 for the tour to the US (and return), and $19,400 as profits for the travel agency. The travel agency in Tianjin asked another travel agency in Beijing to help us to obtain the travel documents, and the Beijing agency asked the Tianjin agency to pay them $12,000 per delegate as collateral. This money would be returned to the Tianjin agency by the Beijing agency after we return to China. The Tianjin agency promised to return $3,600 to us per person after they receive the deposit from the Beijing agency. After that, we can take another trip to the US and stay for good.

The itinerary of our delegation was: Hawaii, Los Angeles, San Diego, Las Vegas, New York, San Francisco, and back to China. After we arrived in New York, we stayed in a hotel in New Jersey. Some time later, the man from Tianjin and I took a taxi from the front of our hotel and told the driver to take us to New York City, to the corner of 42nd Street and 8th Avenue. The driver charged us $100. When we got there, we were met by a friend of mine who took us to her place in Flushing. (The man from Tianjin left the next day and went to Pennsylvania.)

To save money, many groups from China stay in New Jersey hotels while they visit New York. The intersection of 42nd Street and 8th Avenue is where the bus station is located; it is a well-known destination but also one of the most congested places in Manhattan.

After I left the group, someone from the Tianjin agency called me right away. My cell phone was installed with an international calling plan so he could reach me. I told him because it was so hard to enter America I decided not to go back and I did not need that $3,600. Of course he was mad at me. He also went to that Tianjin man's home, but his wife did not know how to contact her husband. He threatened her and said that he would report us to the US immigration office. Fuck the son of a bitch!

Anita was furious when she recalled how her travel agency demanded that she rejoin her group, and she repeatedly cursed those people at the agency.

These people from the travel agency are, strictly speaking, snakeheads [human smugglers], and yet they wanted to report us to the authorities.[2] They should feel lucky that we don't tell the authorities about them. Of course, the Tianjin agency made $8,500 less because we did not go back. The Beijing agency would not return the $12,000 deposit. This means the Tianjin agency made only $7,400 from each delegate who fled.

Working as a Nanny

I began to feel nervous again, thinking that if I let Anita go on like this, she would not be able to finish her story. So I urged her to tell me about what happened after she settled down in the United States.

After arriving in New York, I found a job as a nanny through a newspaper ad. I worked for a Taiwanese family in Manhattan. My monthly income was $1,500. I worked six days a week; on my day off, I left their apartment Saturday night and returned by 8:00 p.m. Sunday. I worked there for only forty days. Let me tell you why. I went to a casino in Connecticut with a friend one weekend.[3] I missed my bus when I was set to return, so I took the next bus and by the time I got back to New York it was almost ten in the evening. On my way back, I received a call from that Taiwanese woman I was working for and she said there is no need for me to come back. My God! It was very cold that night, and I really did not know where to go. I told myself, "I spent $25,400 to come to the United States, yet I am subjected to such humiliation." I felt so bad.

Anita began to cry. I tried to calm her down, all the while worrying that Mary might hear Anita sobbing.

The next day, I went back to pick up my belongings. The Taiwanese couple paid me what they owed me. Two days later, I made another call to a massage parlor. To my surprise, the owner became mad when he realized it was me again. I had called him a few times already when I was working as a nanny. He asked me to go to his place for an interview, and I had never showed up. This time when I called, he told me if I want to work for him, go to his place, if not, don't call anymore.

I went to see him. Once I got there, he asked me to start working right away. My first customer was a man from Hong Kong. I was very stupid then, not knowing that I should ask the customer to wear a condom. Probably because of this, he gave me a $30 tip. When a client walks in, he has to pay $160 for sex. The house takes $70, and I get $90. So I made $120 on my first job.

When Anita turned to the issue of money, she was smiling again. When they talked about their first sexual transaction, some subjects cried and some laughed; every sex worker has a very different feeling and reaction to her first encounter with a client.

After a month in that first massage parlor, I went to work for another parlor. The charge at the second place was the same as the first. However, I also asked a man to help me put an ad on the Internet. In that second parlor, I was seeing Chinese clients who found me through an ad in the Chinese newspapers, but also foreigners who located me through the ad on the Internet. The owner of the second parlor later discovered that I was seeing foreigners without his knowledge, and he was pissed off. I had no choice but to pay him $3,000 to settle this thing. The owner was a Fuzhounese, and those people are really bad, so it was not good for me to be at odds with him.

After that, I only entertained clients in my own place. All my clients found me through the ad on the Internet. I charged the same amount of money ($160). I took $90 and that man who assisted me with the Internet, $70.

I could understand that there was some kind of problem when Anita was working for the second massage parlor and was also being helped with advertising on the Internet, but I did not ask her to elaborate.

One day in April this year, FBI agents busted into my place and arrested me. I was not seeing clients at that time, but they did not care, because they had already been there before, pretending to be sex buyers. That was my first arrest, so they charged me with engagement in lewd conduct, fined me $340, and then let me go. I believe I must have offended a customer, who reported me to the police, and I was arrested. After that incident, I did not work for a month.

I knew I was running out of time, so I asked Anita to talk about her current situation.

This place is a massage parlor and there are only two women working at any given time. I work here only Wednesday and Saturday; I work three days a week at another massage parlor. So I work five days a week. I am still living in Flushing. The massage parlors provide me with rides everyday.

Sending Money Home to Be at Peace

I asked Anita a few questions about money, and also some questions about her clients.

I had to pay the Tianjin travel agency the entire $23,000 before I left China. My elder sister lent me most of the money; my husband only chipped in $3,600. So far, I have already repaid my sister.

Here, a client pays $50 once he walks in, and that money is for the massage. If a client asks for a hand job at the end of the massage, he will give me approximately a $50 tip. If sex, $100. I make about $5,000 a month, and I send most of the money back to China. This is such an unbearable job, I can be at peace only by sending money home.

After interviewing Anita, I returned to the massage parlor a few times in the following days to interview other women. I also told Mary I was actually interviewing her masseuses for my research project. Only later did I learn how Mary was running her business: If a client visits her place for the first time, she will only ask the client to pay $50 for massage and let the masseuse decide whether to offer special service to the client after observing how the client reacts to her hints for special service. If a client is a regular visitor, Mary will charge the person $120 upon arrival, assuming the client is there for sex, and ask him whether he had his own condom. If not, Mary will provide him with one.

> It is hard to say how many clients I see a day. On average, I would say about two or three clients a day. I have Chinese as well as foreign clients; some want a hand job and some want sex. Except for a few bad clients, most are fine. Of course, having sex with clients is not the same as having sex with a husband. As clients, they are demanding.
>
> I regret coming here, and I should not have entered prostitution. To be honest with you, my stomach is filled with bitterness.

At that point, Mary was knocking at the door, saying that my time was up. When I came out, Mary greeted me with a big smile and led me to the door. She also repeatedly asked me to come back again. On my way out, I bumped into a middle-aged Chinese man, and from the way he and Mary talked, I could tell he must be a regular client. Because business was good, Mary was in a good mood.

CHAPTER 18

Climbing Mountains to Enter the United States

CANDY IN NEW YORK

Date: January 1, 2008
Place: An apartment in Flushing (Queens), New York
Name: Candy
Age: 41
Marital Status: Married, with a nineteen-year-old son and seventeen-year-old adopted daughter

Born in Fuzhou, Fujian. Graduated from elementary school. Began working at fifteen; not happy after marriage. Wanted to come to the United States since 1996, but arrested in all three smuggling attempts. Eventually entered the United States in 2006 via Mexico at cost of more than $70,000. Currently seeing clients in her apartment in Flushing, Queens.

"Is this an easy job? Of course not. But is this a terrible job? That isn't so, either."

❦

The Chinese Sex Trade in New York

After interviewing a few women in massage parlors in New Jersey, I turned my attention to New York. As mentioned above, in New Jersey,

Chinese sex venues mostly tend to be massage parlors, whereas in New York, there are nightclubs, KTVs, saunas, and brothels. There are also many Chinese escorts in New York. Some of them do business only with non-Chinese clients, and some, only with Chinese.

There is also another type of Chinese sex venue in New York: a woman's personal apartment. It is run by an independent sex worker who places an ad in the Chinese newspapers, answers the phone herself, and provides sexual service in her place. This type of venue did not exist in the past, but now it has become, along with massage parlors, one of the two major types of sex establishments involving Chinese in the United States.

One day, the following ad in the *World Journal* newspaper caught my eye:

Endless Passion
Soft and Lovely
Excellent body shape
Flushing; Only one client at a time
Free Parking
xxx-xxx-xxxx

In New York, most of these one-woman brothels exist in Manhattan's Chinatown and Flushing and Elmhurst in Queens. I called the phone number in the ad, and a woman answered the phone. After a brief conversation, I asked her how much she charged, and she said a hundred dollars. I asked her where she was located, and she told me her place was not far from Flushing's Chinatown. I drove to her place right away, parked my car at a parking lot she said she had an arrangement with, and called her again. Only then did she give me her apartment number.

Her place was a studio on the first floor of a large apartment building. Once I stepped inside the apartment, I told her about my research project and asked her to participate in my study. She said, "Well, since you are here, it is going to be hard for me to reject your request; I am willing to be interviewed." When I heard that, I was not sure how cooperative she was going to be, but it turned out to be a good interview.

Candy from Fuzhou

When I entered her place, she asked me to remove my shoes. Her studio was clean and orderly. After we both sat down, I asked her to introduce herself.

My name is Candy, and I was born in Fuzhou. I am forty-one now, married, and I have two children. I have a son, and he is nineteen, and an adopted daughter, age seventeen. In China, we can only give birth to one child.

In the mid-1990s, I conducted a study on the smuggling of Chinese from Fuzhou into the United States, and had written a book about it,[1] so I am relatively familiar with what they have to go through to arrive in the United States. I thought that it would be important for me to include a woman from Fuzhou in this study because there are so many anecdotal reports about how smuggled women from Fuzhou are forced into prostitution to repay their exorbitant smuggling fee.

My parents are both farmers, and I had two elder brothers and a younger brother. I only completed elementary school. I wanted to continue with my education, but I did not pass the exam to enter middle school. As a student, I did not have good grades, and whenever I was in class, I got dizzy. I do not know why.

When I was fifteen, I went to work in a shoe factory, making less then $10 a month. After a few years, I quit and opened a barber shop, but after I got married and gave birth, I closed the store. My husband was a worker at a seafood company; he attended elementary school for only one year, so he was poorly educated and uncultured, even worse than me.

After our son was born, my husband and I began to argue often because he became a gambler and a womanizer. He would hit my son in a ferocious way; he would tie him up and then flog him with a belt. My son was so badly beaten that his entire body was covered with wounds. I decided to leave him and come to America.

There were tears in Candy's eyes when she talked about how her husband abused their son.

Sneaking into the United States

I had been trying to come to the US since 1996. I tried and failed three times. The first time I was turned back at the airport in Beijing. The second time I was arrested in South Korea and sent back to China. The third time I was trying to go to Bangkok via Myanmar, but I was arrested in Jinghong, Yunnan Province. The police there accused me of illegal migration, and sent me back to Fuzhou. At Fuzhou, the authorities asked me to pay them $3,000. According to them, of this amount, $1,800 was bail money to ensure that I wouldn't sneak out of China in the next five years. I was supposed to get the money back after five years, but so far I haven't had the chance to get it back.

Candy told me in detail about the three failed attempts to go to the United States, and even though those incidents had occurred many years earlier, she could still recall vividly what had happened on those trips. When Candy tried for the third time, she went through the Golden Triangle of northern Burma. It was clear how desperate she was to get to America. I spent half a year in the Golden Triangle for another research project, and I can fully understand how difficult it is to travel to Bangkok from Jinhong overland via the Golden Triangle, especially if a person is traveling clandestinely.[2]

The three failed attempts cost me a lot of money, and delayed my arrival in the United States by ten years. When I gave it a try the first time, my children were very young, but when I arrived in the United States on my fourth attempt, they had all grown up. Because it took ten years for me to get here, my relatives and friends in Fuzhou could not believe that I had such bad luck. I even joked about this, telling them definitely the US does not want a person like me; otherwise how come it was so hard for me to get there?

Candy seemed to be forcing herself to laugh about all this, and I couldn't help but admire her sense of humor after things had gone terribly wrong on her first three attempts. When Candy tried for the fourth time, she succeeded, even though she not only suffered a lot in the process but also had to pay a lot more money.

A snakehead [human smuggler] in Fuzhou helped me with this last and fourth trip. I traveled for more than fifty days to get here because I had to go through many countries, plus I was stuck in Venezuela for more than a month. Eventually, I sneaked into America from Mexico. When I was smuggled across the border, I was hidden inside a truck with a Chinese man at one point. We could not even move. The engine was right beneath us and it was hot as hell. We were tortured for more than seven hours like that. Later, we walked and climbed mountains. I will never forget that experience, nor would want to go through this ever again. It was really hard.

I am applying for political asylum. I entered the US around August 2006. Before I left China, I agreed to pay the snakehead $73,000 after I arrived in the US. All the money was borrowed money. I had to pay one percent per month interest for some of the borrowed money, and one and a half percent per month interest for the rest. I also owed someone another $12,500 when my husband's business went bankrupt. When I got here, I was paying more than $760 a month in interest alone. Even now, I still owe more than $30,000.

Seeing Clients in Her Own Place

It is incredible that a person who pays $73,000 to come to the United States also has to suffer for more than fifty days on the way.

After I got here, I found a job as a nanny. I took care of two children for a Fuzhounese family, and I was paid $1,500 a month. It was hard work and the kids were not easy to handle. I worked for four months and then decided to become a sex worker. Someone I knew taught me how to find an apartment, how to put an ad in the newspapers, and how to answer phone calls.

When I was in China, I thought that I would work in a restaurant after arriving in the United States; it never crossed my mind that I would become a sex worker. I am from a good family, and I used to look down on those women in the sex trade. Who would have thought that I would become one of them? But I was under a lot of pressure to repay my debt, plus working as a nanny was tough and I did not make much money. From reading the newspapers, we all know that there are places like this [one-woman brothel] in New York. If someone helps us, we can do it ourselves.

When Candy recalled how she used to despise women in the sex business, she flashed a bitter smile.

My first place was also located in Flushing. I contacted a real estate broker to find me a place first, and then put an ad in the World Journal for $170 a month and asked a friend to teach me how to pronounce the English names of the streets around that area. This is my second place; I've been here for six months. The first place's rent was $800 a month; this place costs me $1,000 a month. My monthly expenses mainly include rent, advertisement fee, and parking lot fee; it costs me at least $2,000 a month altogether.

Learning by Working

Even though Candy's current place was a studio, it was relatively large, and that was probably why she needed to pay $1,000 a month for rent. She had to learn the street names because to run the business on her own and answer the phone herself, she needed to at least know how to tell the callers the names of the streets around her place; otherwise, it would not be possible for anyone to locate her. I asked Candy how she runs her business in general.

After a customer walks in, he will take a shower first. Some customers will ask me to take a shower with them, and I will always say no because that's too much. After the shower, I will massage him for a few minutes, and then do it. Actually, I learn a lot of things while working; sometimes clients will also teach me how to do it.

I am doing this all by myself. This is the best arrangement because it is safer and you need not share the money with other people. If you work for other people, you are more likely to be arrested, and the boss is going to take a cut of $30 to $40 per session. If you work on your own, you have more freedom as well.

I asked Candy how much she was making a month.

I charge $100 per job, and I keep all the money. Some clients will give me tips of about $20. People who give me tips are mostly Cantonese (people from Hong Kong and Guangdong Province) and Taiwanese; men from other parts of China do not give tips.

In the past, I netted about $6,000 to $7,000 a month after deducting all my expenses. Now, business is very slow. Today, you are the first visitor. Yesterday, I only had two clients. I can only make a profit of about $4,500 a month now.

In New York and New Jersey, most Chinese women in commercial sex charge from $80 to $150 per session. Those who charge $80 are in general not young anymore. I remember interviewing a fifty-five-year-old Chinese woman in New York who told me she had several grandchildren. Those who charge $150 are younger and prettier. Many Chinese workers who cannot afford to pay $80 will buy sex in places owned by Chinese but staffed with women from Central America simply because these places charge only $35 to $40 per session.

I send all my money home to repay the debt. I am very frugal; I do not smoke, drink, or gamble. My husband is not working; he stays home and does some farming on the side.

Every day, I work from around eleven in the morning until midnight. Many women in the business work only until eight or nine in the evening. I have to repay my debt, so I must work harder. I live here, and I rarely go outside. I am very cautious, and I won't do anything to annoy my neighbors. As long as they don't call the police, I won't be in trouble.

It's not easy to say how many clients I see everyday. Some days, I do not have even one client. Some days, one to two. In a good day, I will see three to four. My clients are fine, they won't ask me to do something I don't want to do. One out of ten will request not to wear a condom, but if I talk to him, he will wear one. Three or four out of ten clients are Cantonese or Taiwanese, the rest are Chinese from other regions of China. I like doing business with Cantonese and Taiwanese because they are of better quality. I especially do not like Fuzhounese customers, even though I am a Fuzhounese myself.

The doorbell rang, and she got up. After Candy opened the wooden door from the inside, there was an outer steel door with bars at the top so she could see the person outside. A man was standing outside—probably someone who had called Candy earlier. After the man took a good look at her, he turned around and left without saying a word. Candy just closed the door and walked back with a smile.

Being rejected is normal because it happens every day. Some men show up and once they see me, they walk away. I don't blame them. Every man has a certain type of woman in mind; so he can reject a woman for being too old or too young, too tall or too short. Every man has his own taste.

I asked Candy whether she had ever been robbed while conducting her business.

What scares me the most is being robbed, but I am also afraid of being arrested. Over the past twelve months, I was robbed three or four times. When I was robbed the first time, my place had been open for only a month. A young Wenzhounese [person from Wenzhou, Zhejiang] walked in and after he was sure I was all by myself, called his partners and let them in. Altogether, there were four of them, and they took $500 and two cell phones. They also ransacked my place. Not long after that, I was robbed by a group of Fuzhounese. After the first incident, I had gotten smarter; I didn't keep a lot of cash in my place. As a result, the Fuzhounese did not find much money, and so they gang raped me. I did not dare call the police.

I asked her about her plans for the future.

> I am applying for political asylum. I want to stay in the United States. I will work for three or four more years in this business; I will repay my debt and save enough money to open a restaurant or a store. I can't be doing sex work forever!

What Can I Do in China?

Candy's eyes were bright with joy when she talked about saving money and opening a restaurant, as if suddenly full of hope for her future. Finally, I asked Candy how she felt about selling sex.

> I do not regret coming here, even if I knew beforehand that I would enter prostitution after arriving here. If I had stayed in China, what could I do?
> Is this an easy job? Of course not. But is this a terrible job? That isn't so, either. If I don't run into a bad client, it is not that hard to do. If I have to deal with a bad client, not only will I be unhappy that entire day, it will linger on for the next few days. That's why when someone calls, I pay particular attention to the caller's voice; if he sounds like a young man, I won't do business with him. Even if a man is at the door, and when I open the door and find out he is a young man, I will shut the door right away. I also don't do business with foreigners; they could be cops.

It was around six in the evening when the interview was completed. I took out a one hundred dollar bill and gave it to her, and she thanked me and accepted the money.

Epilogue

Between 2006 and 2008, I traveled to many cities in Asia and the United States and interviewed 149 female sex workers originally from China. Here I have recounted the stories of eighteen of these women. It is my hope that their stories, told in their own words, will add to an understanding of why and how they entered the sex trade. As mentioned in the prologue, the main reason why I conducted this study was to find out if Chinese women working in the overseas sex industry are trafficked—deceived, coerced, or forced into prostitution by groups or individuals.

According to the women's accounts, the vast majority of them were not deceived, coerced, or forced into the sex trade abroad. Only Molly in Thailand said that she felt like she was tricked into the sex business by her aunt. However, there were five cases whereby the women (Kitty, Dong Dong, Ruby, Chloe, and Cola) were coerced into prostitution by their boyfriends or chickenheads in China. In these cases, they can be considered as victims of domestic—not transnational—trafficking.

I learned two things from this research. First, depending on how strictly or loosely a person defines sex trafficking, he or she might come up with a significantly different estimate of the numbers of trafficked victims. A very large proportion (about 93 percent) of women interviewed for my original research project could be called trafficking victims if the definition is simply anyone who is assisted in going to another country by another person, regardless of whether the facilitator is paid. If I go by the transportation criterion, which holds that a person is a trafficking victim if sent abroad by a third party or accompanied during their travels, then I find that 74 percent of all the women interviewed fit the definition. Other possible definitions of a sex trafficking victim could be a person who pays a fee for help going abroad (68 percent of my interview subjects fit into this group) and someone who goes overseas in debt to the same person she is going to work for (true for 23 percent of the sex workers interviewed).

If I define a sex trafficking victim as someone who is financially exploited (receives only half or less of what a client pays), 26 percent of my subjects would be considered trafficking victims. This figure becomes 15 percent if a sex trafficking victim is defined as a woman who is not free to move around or quit sex work because her travel documents are kept by her employer or debtor. Under the strictest definition—only counting those who are forced, deceived, or coerced into commercial sex—only 1 percent of the interviewees could be considered trafficking victims.

Second, it is clear to me that the seriousness and nature of human trafficking can be very country-specific. Of all the destination regions or countries for Chinese women in my study, Hong Kong and Macau are different from the others in that women from China can travel to these two special regions with relative ease. However, the women there are also most vulnerable to chickenheads—the men who probably best match the notorious description of "human traffickers."

Chinese sex workers in Taiwan fit most of the definitions mentioned above, but none of the women in Taiwan can be considered trafficking victims under the US government's definition of "severe forms of trafficking in persons." Even so, the plight of Chinese sex workers in Taiwan should not be discounted, as most of the women I interviewed there arrived under debt, were "owned" by agents, were engaged in highly organized commercial sex involving many parties, and were often financially exploited.

Chinese women in the Thai sex sector are most likely to be brought overseas by relatives or neighbors who are returned sex workers, as opposed to agents, brokers, or companies. Thailand has a low rate of human trafficking in terms of almost all the definitions mentioned above, and Chinese women there are least likely to be victimized by sex ring operators. Malaysia, as a destination country, is somewhat unique because Chinese sex workers there are equally involved in both highly organized as well as unorganized commercial sex. This is similar to Singapore, which also has a variety of sex venues available to Chinese women, but because it is a Chinese society and more developed than Malaysia, most Chinese women prefer to go to Singapore. Indonesia, like Taiwan, has a highly organized commercial sex scene and high rates of sex trafficking based on most of the definitions, but unlike in Taiwan, the women in Indonesia must turn in their travel documents when they are hired, regardless of whether they owe road fees to their employers. This system restricts the free movement of the women and increases their vulnerability to financial exploitation.

In the United States, the world leader in the global war against prostitution and human trafficking, the problem of sex trafficking involving Chinese women is less grave than in the Asian countries I researched. The majority of my US interviewees had to pay someone to help them to come to the United States, but none of them were underage, in debt to sex ring operators, financially exploited, denied freedom of movement, or forced, coerced, or deceived into commercial sex. The United States actually ranks very low in sex trafficking based on the definitions above.

Besides the United States, sex trafficking has gained the attention of international groupings like the United Nations and the European Union. One of the reasons for this is that many government officials believe organized crime groups are not only involved in the transportation of women and children but are also directly engaged in buying, selling, and exploiting these victims. Throughout the eighteen accounts in this book, readers should have noticed that there are no dark shadows lurking around as knife-wielding, gun-toting villains. We know that China has many mafia-type organizations, that Hong Kong and Macau have the triads,[1] that Taiwan has organized gangs, and that Singapore and Malaysia have a significant number of Chinese organized gangs. Yet except for contact with gang members working in the Geylang red light district of Singapore, there was never an account by a sex worker stating she had any association with an organized crime group while working overseas.

Due to pressure from the United Nations and the United States, many countries have passed laws for the protection of trafficked victims and have supported measures such as the establishment of ad hoc groups to combat human trafficking and prosecute traffickers. There are also special prosecutors, rescue organizations, shelters, and awareness programs to prevent human trafficking, protect victims, and prosecute traffickers—the so-called "Three Ps" approach to human trafficking. Most governments have widely adopted large-scale raids on sex venues, especially venues or places that have many foreign female workers. As a consequence, many of these venues have moved out of the public eye to underground locations. The best example is Hong Kong. Due to intense law enforcement, the number of visible streetwalkers has reduced significantly; however, these women have not stopped working and have not vanished from Hong Kong. What has happened is that women have hired other women to solicit customers for them, have turned to the one-woman brothel idea, or have begun soliciting business via the Internet.

Various governments' attempts to combat trafficking have only increased the expenses of women who wish to try their luck overseas. The women also end up needing to pay for additional expertise to obtain appropriate travel documents and make the right connections. After arriving in the foreign country, these women will need further local assistance in order to do business and will perhaps be increasingly subjected to debt bondage or restrictions (control). We think that we are combating human trafficking and providing humanitarian aid to victims, yet in reality we might be exacerbating the very problem we are trying to solve. Perhaps, after a decade or more of misjudgment, we should try to understand why these young and not-so-young women are so willing to leave home and travel abroad to sell sex. Only then will we develop policies and measures that really help these women who are selling sex overseas.

Notes

Prologue

1. The research project was supported by Grant No. 2006-IJ-CX-0008, awarded by the National Institute of Justice, Office of Justice Programs, US Department of Justice. The points of view expressed here are solely the author's and do not necessarily represent the official positions or policy of the US Department of Justice.

2. *Xaihai*, or "going down to the sea," here refers to entering prostitution, although the term has been widely used in China since the Mao era when someone quits a salaried job and becomes an entrepreneur. After "going down to the sea," one must swim constantly to stay afloat and to survive, so the term connotes struggle, despair, danger, and uncertainty. Quitting prostitution is called *shangan* ("to swim ashore").

3. A KTV is a karaoke nightclub or establishment with many private rooms where people go to sing, drink, and have fun. While some of them are family-oriented, catering to men, women, and children with no hostesses, other KTVs are fronts for prostitution, where young women working as hostesses will engage in intimate acts with their male clients within the premise and in some cases leave the KTV with their clients to have sex. All KTVs referred to in this book are sex establishments.

4. The academic book *Selling Sex Overseas: Chinese Women and the Realities of Prostitution and Global Sex Trafficking* (cowritten by James O. Finckenauer) was published by New York University Press in 2012. It won the 2013 Outstanding

Book Award from the Division of International Criminology of the American Society of Criminology.

1 Offering the Girlfriend Experience

1. All names of the sex workers and sex ring operators mentioned in this book are pseudonyms.

2. For the sake of convenience, I have converted all foreign currencies (Hong Kong dollars in this case) into American dollars. Because of the fluctuations in exchange rates, the US dollar amounts presented had to be ballpark estimates. The conversion also accounts for why the amounts cited are often seemingly very specific.

3. DUP rhymes with the Cantonese (the dialect spoken by people in Hong Kong and Guangdong Province) word for massage, HJ means hand job, ML means make love, and "full set" refers to sexual intercourse plus fellatio.

4. A one-woman brothel is legal in Hong Kong as long as there is only one woman and one man inside the room and no third party is involved in the transaction or benefits from it.

5. Chongqing is a major city in southwest China and one of the four municipalities (along with Beijing, Shanghai, and Tianjin) directly under the central government.

6. There are large numbers of so-called *falang* (hair salons) in China and some hair salons are actually legitimate businesses that provide haircuts and shampoos, facial care and facial massages, and sometimes body massages. However, there are also many hair salons that are essentially brothels (and some that provide both licit and illicit services) to mostly working-class males. These sex venues are most likely to be targeted whenever there is a crackdown on prostitution.

7. Changping is a small industrial town located in Dongguan, a prefecture-level city in central Guangdong Province. Dongguan is known as China's "sex capital" because it has the largest commercial sex sector in China.

8. After China adopted its open-door policy in the late 1970s, the Chinese government selected Shenzhen, a small town adjacent to Hong Kong, as the first special economic zone in China. After more than three decades of mind-boggling growth, Shenzhen is now one of the largest (with a population of more than ten million) and most liberal cities in China.

9. There are many checkpoints between Shenzhen and Hong Kong, but the Luohu is the busiest one. People from China with a travel permit simply walk through the various checkpoints to enter Hong Kong.

Notes

2 Sitting Table and Doing "Fast Food"

1. Changan, like Changping, is also part of Dongguan. However, being closer to Shenzhen and Hong Kong than Changping is, Changan has a bigger adult entertainment industry.

2. Mahjong is a popular Chinese game commonly played by four players with a set of 136 tiles based on Chinese characters and symbols.

3 Macau, a Small Hotel, and Chickenheads

1. Zhuhai, with a population of 1.5 million, is located near Macau. Like Shenzhen and Dongguan, it has a well-established commercial sex sector.

4 Deluxe Style in a Sauna

1. I did not explore the differences among the three styles, but I will assume that the types of sex services provided are different for each style.

5 An Agent, a Jockey, and a Fake Husband

1. Taichung is located in Central Taiwan and it is the third largest city in Taiwan, after Taipei and Kaohsiung.

6 Six Trips to Taiwan in Ten Years

1. Pingtan is an island located between mainland China and Taiwan. The island is the administrative seat of one of the poorest counties in China, and it is also a major staging point for the smuggling of Chinese citizens to Taiwan by boat.

7 Earning Tips in a Flower Hall

1. The majority of ethnic Chinese living in Thailand originated from an area in Guangdong Province called Chaozhou.

10 Sex Work in a Food Court

1. Taizhou, population 5.9 million, is the fourth largest city in Zhejiang, after Wenzhou, Hangzhou, and Ningbo.

11 Walking the Streets of Geylang

1. Shenyang is the capital of Liaoning Province. With a population of more than eight million, it is also the largest city in Northeast China and an important industrial center.

13 A One-and-a-Half-Million-Rupiah Spa

1. Fuqing is another city in Fujian Province, like Fuzhou, with a large overseas population. People from Fuqing are more likely to migrate to Europe than the United States.

15 Thinking the Most Romantic Thing

1. These scores are used by American universities to examine a foreign student's abilities in language, mathematics, and analysis.

16 Making $20,000 a Month

1. Foreigners arriving in the United States with non-immigrant visas are allowed to apply for a driver's license. If they overstay their visas, they become ineligible. That is why those who intend to overstay their visas must obtain a driver's license before they are out of status, especially if they are staying in a place like Los Angeles where the public transportation system is not well developed.

2. At one point during my stay in San Gabriel, I had another interview with a house owner. When I was conducting the interview, a man who looked to be in his late fifties walked down from upstairs after completing a sexual transaction. After he paid the house owner and was about to leave, he turned around and complained to the owner that the woman he had just had sex with provided very poor service. He seemed to be very upset. At that moment, the woman in question also came down the stairs and heard what the man was saying. After the man and the woman were both gone, the female house owner told me in a sarcastic tone, "That old man got what he deserved. Who asked him to insist on getting a young and pretty woman? Of course her service is not going to be good. Men are always like this; they complain a lot after sex, not before."

3. The Refugee Act of 1980 makes a person eligible for asylum if he or she has suffered past persecution or has a well-founded fear of persecution on account of race, religion, nationality, membership in a particular political group, or political opinion. Most smuggled Chinese immigrants apply for political asylum after arriving in the United States, claiming they were persecuted under the one-child policy or because of their religion.

17 More than Massage in a Massage Parlor

1. New York City has five boroughs: Manhattan, Queens, Brooklyn, Bronx, and Staten Island. Most Chinese immigrants live in the first three boroughs.

2. In China, illegal immigrants are called "snake people," and their smugglers, "snakeheads."

3. Most people in the tri-state area of New York, New Jersey, and Connecticut go to either Atlantic City in New Jersey or the two major casinos in Connecticut to gamble.

18 Climbing Mountains to Enter the United States

1. Ko-lin Chin, *Smuggled Chinese: Clandestine Immigration to the United States*, Philadelphia: Temple University Press, 1999.

2. Readers who are interested in the drug trade in the Golden Triangle can take a look at a book I wrote, *The Golden Triangle: Inside Southeast Asia Drug Trade* (Ithaca: Cornell University Press, 2009).

Epilogue

1. Triad societies in Hong Kong are alleged to be some of the largest, most dangerous, and best organized crime groups in the world. The word "triad" means the unity of three essential elements of existence: heaven, earth, and humanity. In the early 1990s, there were roughly 160,000 triad members in Hong Kong, belonging to some fifty factions. Nowadays, only fourteen out of the fifty triad societies remain active, and of these, Sun Yee On, Wo Shing Wo, and 14K are the most powerful organizations.